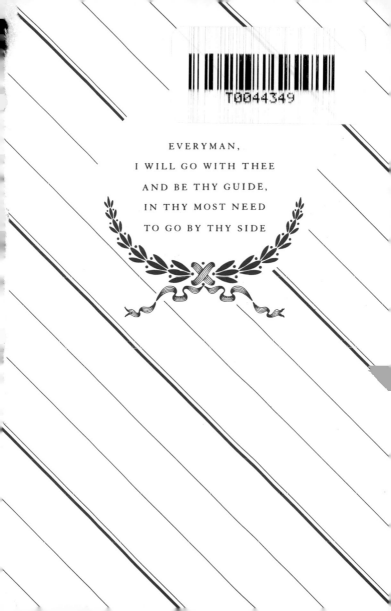

T0044349

BOOKS AND LIBRARIES

POEMS

••••••••••••••••••

EDITED BY
ANDREW D. SCRIMGEOUR

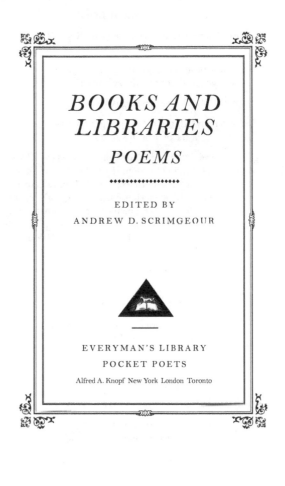

EVERYMAN'S LIBRARY
POCKET POETS

Alfred A. Knopf New York London Toronto

THIS IS A BORZOI BOOK
PUBLISHED BY ALFRED A. KNOPF

This selection by Andrew D. Scrimgeour
first published in Everyman's Library, 2021
Copyright © 2021 by Everyman's Library

Third printing (US)

A list of acknowledgments to copyright owners appears
at the back of this volume.

All rights reserved. Published in the United States by Alfred A.
Knopf, a division of Penguin Random House LLC, New York, and
in Canada by Penguin Random House Canada Limited, Toronto.
Distributed by Penguin Random House LLC, New York. Published
in the United Kingdom by Everyman's Library, 50 Albemarle
Street, London W1S 4BD and distributed by Penguin Random
House UK, 20 Vauxhall Bridge Road, London SW1V 2SA.

www.randomhouse.com/everymans
www.everymanslibrary.co.uk

ISBN 978-0-593-32019-8 (US)
978-1-84159-823-9 (UK)

A CIP catalogue record for this book is available
from the British Library

Typography by Peter B. Willberg

Typeset in the UK by Input Data Services Ltd, Isle Abbotts, Somerset

Printed and bound in Germany
by GGP Media GmbH, Pössneck

CONTENTS

7

9

PREFACE

Ever since Johannes Gutenberg transformed the printing of books, making them available to a wider public, books have captured the imaginations of readers everywhere, inspiring love, and even veneration. Indeed, books may be unrivaled in evoking such bone-deep affection. William Wordsworth said that these page-packed parcels have wings to take us 'as far as we can go', to 'wilderness and wood, / Blank ocean and mere sky'. For Alberto Ríos, they are 'the deli offerings of civilization itself'. When you enter a room full of books, even if you don't take one off the shelf, W. E. Gladstone observed, 'they seem to speak to you, to bid you welcome'.

They also ask to be handled. As Rosemary Griebel put it, books wait 'like abandoned dogs / for the warmth of hands on their spines'. Books are meant to be caressed, page by page, with a gentle downward motion, sometimes with a touch of moisture from the forefinger, as the reader leans attentively over them.

Books awaken all the senses, and many people name the sweet, musty autumn scent in libraries and used bookstores as among their favorites, along with freshly cut grass and bread baking in the oven. Robert Chapman evokes that olfactory delight: 'Amidst the sweets and / Dust of the stacks / I edge from book to book like a grimy kid, / Flattening his nose against an infinitude / Of candy store and bake shop fronts.'

So we line our walls with them, spend the milk money on them, read them aloud, converse with them, argue with them, annotate them, learn from them, raid them, edit them, translate them, write more of them, and fail to winnow them – reaping the displeasure of our spouses and partners who threaten to turn us out of our book-crammed homes.

Our adulation of books naturally extends to the consummate book *place* – the library. We remember and honor the awe-inspiring reading rooms with their stained glass, inexhaustible holdings, and sequestered places in the stacks where, with Billy Collins, one might hear 'a choir of authors murmuring inside their books / along the unlit, alphabetical shelves'.

Over the years as a dean of libraries, I loved being alone in the library at night after closing, especially in winter as snow fell. The library in its serene stillness had the feel of a snug greenhouse – a place where words slumbered like seeds in their stiff covers, awaiting the warmth of our hands to awaken them and bring to flower the tales of novelists, the arguments of philosophers, and the diggings of historians.

Not only are libraries the memory banks of civilization, they are symbolic sanctuaries of the freedom of a people to speak its mind. In the stacks a cacophony of voices is heard on every side of an issue, voices from the past and the present, from the center of the dominant culture and from the margins. The iconic figures of the past are routinely studied, interrogated, decried, demoted, deconstructed, and revered – but never silenced or discarded. Minor ones and neglected ones are constantly discovered and rediscovered and promoted to principal interlocutors in scholarly discourse. Even the most hostile voices are accorded the same protected space. 'If librarians were honest,' writes Joseph Mills, 'They would post danger / signs warning that contact / might result in mood swings, / severe changes in vision, / and mind-altering effects'.

Joining the tributes to libraries are those that honor librarians – the ones who welcomed the poets in their formative years into the world of books; who, as Nikki Giovanni says, first 'opened that wardrobe / But no lions or witches scared me'; dependable guides who over the years encouraged them to go deeper into the stacks and take an armload of adventure home, where it might be enjoyed deep into the night under the covers with a flashlight.

The poets gathered here range from the author of Ecclesiastes in the third century BCE to canonical writers of British, American, and Spanish literature such as William Shakespeare, Emily Dickinson, and Pablo Neruda. Strongly represented are contemporary poets writing in countries across many time zones. Some are well known throughout the world, others enjoy regional status, and a few are published here for the first time. The love of books and libraries knows no linguistic boundaries, so a third of these poems have been rendered in translation. Interestingly, a number of the poets included have themselves been librarians, J. W. von Goethe, Coventry Patmore, Jorge Luis Borges, Philip Larkin and Rosemary Griebel amongst them.

I should like to dedicate this volume to Alexander Lukens, Jr., Katherine W. McCain, Virginia Ramsey Mollenkott, Kent Harold Richards, Deborah Strong, Howard D. White and Louis Charles Willard for debts untold.

Finally, as you embark on an excursion through these pages, a toast:

> May the bookshelves on your walls be full
> May the book stacks on your desk
> and by your chair or bed be high
> And may the doors of your library
> remain open – always.

Godspeed.

Andrew D. Scrimgeour

THE LOVE OF BOOKS

THE HOUSE WAS QUIET AND THE WORLD WAS CALM

The house was quiet and the world was calm.
The reader became the book; and summer night

Was like the conscious being of the book.
The house was quiet and the world was calm.

The words were spoken as if there was no book,
Except that the reader leaned above the page,

Wanted to lean, wanted much most to be
The scholar to whom his book is true, to whom

The summer night is like a perfection of thought.
The house was quiet because it had to be.

The quiet was part of the meaning, part of the mind:
The access of perfection to the page.

And the world was calm. The truth in a calm world,
In which there is no other meaning, itself

Is calm, itself is summer and night, itself
Is the reader leaning late and reading there.

From NOTES ON THE ART OF POETRY

I could never have dreamt that there were such goings-on in the world between the covers of books, such sandstorms and ice blasts of words . . . or such slashing of humbug, and humbug too, such staggering peace, such enormous laughter, such and so many blinding bright lights . . . or breaking across the just-awaking wits and splashing all over the pages in a million bits and pieces all of which were words, words, words, and each of which was alive forever in its own delight and glory and oddity and light.

TO HIS LIBRARY HAVING BEENE
SOMETIME ABSENT THENCE

Salvete incolumes mei Libelli,
Meæ deliciæ, mei lepores, &c.

Hayle to my bookes safe and in sight.
You, all my mirth; my choice delight.
My *Cicero* and *Plinies* both,
All haile to you; whom I was loath
To leave one minut: *Cato, Columel,*
My *Varro, Livy,* all are well.
Hayle to my *Plautus, Terence* too,
And *Ovid* say, how dost thou doe?
My *Fabius,* my *Propertius,*
And those not least belov'd of us,
Greeke Authors, exquisite all o're,
And whom I should have nam'd before,
Because of their Cothurnat straine,
And *Homer* then, whom not in vaine,
The people stil'd great: next I see
My *Aristotle,* hayle to thee
Plato, Tymæus, and the rest
Of you who cannot be exprest
In a phaleucik number; all,
Hayle to my Bookes in generall
Againe, and thrice, againe all hayle,

And may my prayer thus far prevaile,
O you my best lov'd bookes I pray,
(For I have beene sixe dayes away)
My absence yee will not distaste,
But with this love I left you last
You will receive me, which I vow,
Was fervent and sincere to you,
And if you grant this small request,
I further unto you protest,
Henceforth from you Ile be away
No weeke, no weeke said I? no day,
No day? no houre shall loose my care,
No minutes space that I can spare.

THEODORE BEZA
      TRANSLATED BY THOMAS HEYWOOD

PERSONAL TALK AND BOOKS

Wings have we, and as far as we can go
We may find pleasure: wilderness and wood,
Blank ocean and mere sky, support that mood
Which with the lofty sanctifies the low:
Dreams, books, are each a world; and books, we know,
Are a substantial world, both pure and good:
Round these, with tendrils strong as flesh and blood,
Our pastime and our happiness will grow.
There find I personal themes, a plenteous store,
Matter wherein right voluble am I,
To which I listen with a ready ear.
Two shall be named, pre-eminently dear: –
The gentle Lady married to the Moor,
And heavenly Una with her milk-white Lamb.

'THERE IS NO FRIGATE LIKE A BOOK'

There is no Frigate like a Book
To take us Lands away
Nor any Coursers like a Page
Of prancing Poetry –
This Traverse may the poorest take
Without oppress of Toll –
How frugal is the Chariot
That bears the Human soul –

SONNET XXIII

As an unperfect actor on the stage,
Who with his fear is put besides his part,
Or some fierce thing replete with too much rage,
Whose strength's abundance weakens his own heart;
So I, for fear of trust, forget to say
The perfect ceremony of love's rite,
And in mine own love's strength seem to decay,
O'ercharged with burden of mine own love's might.
O, let my books be then the eloquence
And dumb presagers of my speaking breast,
Who plead for love, and look for recompense,
More than that tongue that more hath more
     expressed.
  O, learn to read what silent love hath writ.
  To hear with eyes belongs to love's fine wit.

From THE LIBRARY

But what strange art, what magic can dispose
The troubled mind to change its native woes?
Or lead us willing from ourselves, to see
Others more wretched, more undone than we?
This BOOKS can do; – nor this alone; they give
New views to life, and teach us how to live;
They soothe the grieved, the stubborn they chastise,
Fools they admonish, and confirm the wise:
Their aid they yield to all: they never shun
The man of sorrow, nor the wretch undone:
Unlike the hard, the selfish, and the proud,
They fly not sullen from the suppliant crowd;
Nor tell to various people various things,
But show to subjects what they show to kings.

UNACCOMPANIED MINOR
Section 26, Kakuma Refugee Camp, Kenya 1996
after Robert Lyons, with Chinua Achebe

Stand still in the hot shade, poised, sweatless.
See how the curtain sifts sand from sun
through paisley print.
See five orange lozenges
paint light onto his profile.

The thinker: here is a boy whose thighs have
    outgrown him.
Soon this neatly striped Old Navy shirt will not fit
    him either.

Notice that his shoes are still new enough
to stamp a grid on each resting place.
Let sentiment blur the outlines of a rondavel
through the curtain. Read a word, MASKANI,
    stamped
in stark, block capitals, as if on a ticket.

Fuss at the curtain, a veil against flies.
Count the trees here, as you lean against geometry.
Catch them catching the light, as you square the
    threshold.
Sense the slope of his cottoned shoulders,

the dance of print on skin. Know
his eyes are unquiet.
What is the name of the book in his hands,
his sanctum's seam, that wild unaccompanied
outer world, whose hem you may not mend?
Camp here, in this dwelling.

I LOVE THE LOOK OF WORDS

Popcorn leaps, popping from the floor
of a hot black skillet
and into my mouth.
Black words leap,
snapping from the white
page. Rushing into my eyes. Sliding
into my brain which gobbles them
the way my tongue and teeth
chomp the buttered popcorn.

When I have stopped reading,
ideas from the words stay stuck
in my mind, like the sweet
smell of butter perfuming my
fingers long after the popcorn
is finished.

I love the book and the look of words
the weight of ideas that popped into my mind
I love the tracks
of new thinking in my mind.

MAYA ANGELOU   29

LATIN PROVERB

Verba volant,
scripta manent

Spoken words fly away,
written words remain

From IN PRAISE OF LIBRARIES

Seven

In convents and crypts, in kists and coffins,
tiny illuminations;
in private collections chained and padlocked
or dusty, oak-panelled institutions
where sunlight canticles on a spine,
a gold-leafed title: *The Golden Bough*;
or moonlight charms the pallor of
a forgotten *Woman in White*;
or a girl from the country slits apart
a thick, warm page of cavorting Sanskrit;
or on paper as thin as a butterfly wing
holds a pocketbook of proverbs.

Books, too precious to keep,
too tough to destroy, too
dangerous to trust, too
charged with truth, too
silent in face of violence, too
volatile for the screen, books
are thoughts in transit, they gather
as they go more and more rolling beauty.
Who knows who shall know?
Whom will the finger touch?

TESSA RANSFORD

TO HIS BOOKS

Bright books! the perspectives to our weak sights,
The clear projections of discerning lights,
Burning and shining thoughts, man's posthume day,
The track of fled souls, and their milkie way,
The dead alive and busie, the still voice
Of enlarged spirits, kind Heaven's white decoys!
Who lives with you lives like those knowing flowers,
Which in commerce with light spend all their hours;
Which shut to clouds, and shadows nicely shun,
But with glad haste unveil to kiss the sun.
Beneath you all is dark, and a dead night,
Which whoso lives in wants both health and sight.
   By sucking you, the wise, like bees, do grow
Healing and rich, though this they do most slow,
Because most choicely; for as great a store
Have we of books as bees of herbs, or more:
And the great task to try, then know, the good,
To discern weeds, and judge of wholesome food,
Is a rare scant performance. For man dyes
Oft ere 'tis done, while the bee feeds and flyes.
But you were all choice flowers; all set and dressed
By old sage florists, who well knew the best;

And I amidst you all am turned a weed,
Not wanting knowledge, but for want of heed.
Then thank thyself, wild fool, that wouldst not be
Content to know – what was too much for thee!

VALEDICTION TO HIS BOOKE

I'll tell thee now (deare Love) what thou shalt doe
   To anger destiny, as she doth us,
   How I shall stay, though she Esloygne me thus
And how posterity shall know it too;
     How thine may out-endure
     Sybills glory, and obscure
     Her who from Pindar could allure,
   And her, through whose helpe *Lucan* is not lame,
And her, whose booke (they say) *Homer* did finde,
       and name.

Study our manuscripts, those Myriades
   Of letters, which have past twixt thee and mee,
   Thence write our Annals, and in them will bee
To all whom loves subliming fire invades,
     Rule and example found;
     There, the faith of any ground
     No schismatique will dare to wound,
   That sees, how Love this grace to us affords,
To make, to keep, to use, to be these his Records,

This Booke, as long-liv'd as the elements,
   Or as the worlds forme, this all-graved tome
   In cypher writ, or new made Idiome;
Wee for loves clergie only'are instruments,

When this booke is made thus,
  Should againe the ravenous
  Vandals and Goths invade us,
 Learning were safe; in this our Universe
Schooles might learne Sciences, Spheares Musick,
   Angels Verse.

Here Loves Divines, (since all Divinity
  Is love or wonder) may finde all they seeke,
  Whether abstract spirituall love they like,
Their Soules exhal'd with what they do not see,
   Or, loth so to amuze,
   Faiths infirmitie, they chuse
   Something which they may see and use;
  For, though minde be the heaven, where love
    doth sit,
Beauty a convenient type may be to figure it.

Here more than in their bookes may Lawyers finde,
  Both by what titles, Mistresses are ours,
  And how prerogative these states devours,
Transferr'd from Love himselfe, to womankinde,
   Who though from heart, and eyes,
   They exact great subsidies,
   Forsake him who on them relies
  And for the cause, honour, or conscience give,
Chimeraes, vaine as they, or their prerogative.

Here Statesmen, (or of them, they which can reade,)
   May of their occupation finde the grounds,
   Love and their art alike it deadly wounds,
If to consider what 'tis, one proceed,
     In both they doe excell
     Who the present governe well,
     Whose weaknesse none doth, or dares tell;
   In this thy booke, such will their nothing see,
As in the Bible some can finde out Alchimy.

Thus vent thy thoughts; abroad I'll studie thee,
   As he removes farre off, that great heights takes;
   How great love is, presence best tryall makes,
But absence tryes how long this love will bee;
     To take a latitude
     Sun, or starres, are fitliest view'd
     At their brightest, but to conclude
   Of longitudes, what other way have wee,
But to marke when, and where the darke eclipses bee?

From ODE TO THE BOOK (II)

Book,
beautiful
book,
minuscule forest,
leaf
after leaf,
your paper
smells
of the elements,
you are
matutinal and nocturnal,
vegetal,
oceanic,
in your ancient pages
bear hunters,
bonfires
near the Mississippi,
canoes
in the islands,
later
roads
and roads,
revelations,
insurgent
races,

Rimbaud like a wounded
fish bleeding
thumping in the mud,
and the beauty
of fellowship,
stone by stone
the human castle rises,
sorrows intertwined
with strength,
actions of solidarity,
clandestine
book
from pocket
to pocket,
hidden
lamp,
red star.

TRANSLATED BY STEPHEN MITCHELL

SWORD DRILL

Boy, girl, boy, girl, boy, girl, that great misery of
    childhood,
worked its torment: the boys on either side of me
whispering to girls on other sides of them,
then glancing at me to decide. *Cat had got my tongue*
and kept it ever since I'd passed the note to Eddie
    Pittman:
Do you still love me? Yes. No. Circle one.
He circled *No*, then chased Cathie Smith at recess,
the girl with thin white straps beneath her shirt.

Now I stared down at the Old Testament's Table of
    Contents,
mouthing the list, the fire on my face drenched only
    when
ATTENTION! jerked the wriggle
of a line of 10-year-olds at Baptist Training Union
to straighten and suck in its breath.
Staring straight ahead, gripping our Swords, we stood
on the stage of the Fellowship Hall, on the dark bank
of the golden river the spotlights poured right in front
    of us.

The church had issued Bibles, stiff as dictionaries
in black cardboard covers – but for luck I held my
     own,
autographed inside by Vince Cevera (the evangelist
     who saved me)
and covered with leather the color of Jesus' words.
Now the *genuine cowhide* was slick with the sweat
of my palm. DRAW SWORDS!
We drew our Bibles up, right hands cradling
the back covers, left hands resting on the fronts,

twenty Bibles hovering, mine red among the black
like a patch of blossom or blood.
I ached to touch the tissue pages,
to get my thumbnail slid inside Isaiah,
but judges watched from their row of straightbacked
chairs behind Miss Swope, who commanded us:
FIRST CORINTHIANS 13:12. REPEAT.
FIRST CORINTHIANS 13:12. CHARGE!

Then all down the line a creak of spines, crackle
of pages, the gulp past prophets, gospels, acts, to the
     lick
of fingers stuck to dry pages almost ripped nearing
chapter, verse, boys' arms grazing girls', mine
     scraping

past theirs as I lurched first into the light, *For now*
we see through a glass, darkly; but then face to face,
    clutching
the coveted words, unsheathed
in time.

BOOK ENDS (I)

Baked the day she suddenly dropped dead
we chew it slowly that last apple pie.

Shocked into sleeplessness you're scared of bed.
We never could talk much, and now don't try.

You're like book ends, the pair of you, she'd say,
Hog that grate, say nothing, sit, sleep, stare . . .

The 'scholar' me, you, worn out on poor pay,
only our silence made us seem a pair.

Not as good for staring in, blue gas,
too regular each bud, each yellow spike.

A night you need my company to pass
and she not here to tell us we're alike!

Your life's all shattered into smithereens.

Back in our silences and sullen looks,
for all the Scotch we drink, what 's still between 's
not the thirty or so years, but books, books, books.

ALL SORTS OF
READERS

From *SEVEN LECTURES ON SHAKESPEARE AND MILTON* (*Second Lecture*)

Readers may be divided into four classes:

1. Sponges, who absorb all they read, and return it nearly in the same state, only a little dirtied.

2. Sand-glasses, who retain nothing, and are content to get through a book for the sake of getting through the time.

3. Strain-bags, who retain merely the dregs of what they read.

4. Mogul diamonds, equally rare and valuable, who profit by what they read, and enable others to profit by it also.

S. T. COLERIDGE

THE BRITISH MUSEUM READING ROOM

Under the hive-like dome the stooping haunted readers
Go up and down the alleys, tap the cells of knowledge –
    Honey and wax, the accumulation of years –
Some on commission, some for the love of learning,
Some because they have nothing better to do
Or because they hope these walls of books will deaden
    The drumming of the demon in their ears.

Cranks, hacks, poverty-stricken scholars,
In pince-nez, period hats or romantic beards
    And cherishing their hobby or their doom,
Some are too much alive and some are asleep
Hanging like bats in a world of inverted values,
Folded up in themselves in a world which is safe and
       silent:
    This is the British Museum Reading Room.

Out on the steps in the sun the pigeons are courting,
Puffing their ruffs and sweeping their tails or taking
    A sun-bath at the ease
And under the totem poles – the ancient terror –
Between the enormous fluted Ionic columns
There seeps from heavily jowled or hawk-like foreign
       faces
    The guttural sorrow of the refugees.

NIGHT SEASONS

Up late, reading alone,
I feed printed pages
Into the Kurzweil scanner,
An electronic reader
For the blind.

Randomly now
I take books from my shelves,
Open the mysterious volumes,
And lay them flat on the machine.
I can't say
What's coming next —
I wait in perfect silence
For the voice to begin,
This synthetic child
Reading to an old man.

The body, stalled,
Picks fragments,
Frottage,
Scraps of paper,
Whatever comes.

Pico della Mirandola,
Egyptian love poems,
Essene communes beside the Red Sea,
Paavo Haavikko's 'König Harald' . . .

An old professor,
Bitter at the graceful way
The poets have
Of gathering terms
Inexactly,
Told me, 'The poets are fools.
They read
Only in fragments.'

I'm the fool
Of the night seasons,
Reading anything, *anything.*
When daylight comes
And you see me on the street
Or standing for the bus,
Think of the Greek term
Entelechy,
Word for soul and body
Constructing each other
After dark.

THE REVELATION

An idle poet, here and there,
   Looks round him; but, for all the rest,
The world, unfathomably fair,
   Is duller than a witling's jest.
Love wakes men, once a lifetime each;
   They lift their heavy lids, and look;
And, lo, what one sweet page can teach,
   They read with joy, then shut the book.
And some give thanks, and some blaspheme
   And most forget; but, either way,
That and the Child's unheeded dream
Is all the light of all their day.

COVENTRY PATMORE

ON HIS BOOKS

When I am dead, I hope it may be said:
'His sins were scarlet, but his books were read.'

From A DESCRIPTION OF A COLLEGE ROOM

. . . While various books confus'dly lie,
Scotch songs, with deep *philosophy*,
A *Prior* here, and *Euclid* there,
A *Rochester* and *book of prayer*;
Here *Tillotson* with *French romances*,
And pious *South* with *country dances* . . .

TO HIS VALET

I want three days to read the Iliad through!
    So, Corydon, close fast my chamber door.
    If anything should bother me before
I've done, I swear you'll have somewhat to rue!

No! not the servant, nor your mate, nor you
    Shall come to make the bed or clean the floor.
    I must have three good quiet days – or four.
Then I'll make merry for a week or two.

Ah! but – if any one should come from HER,
    Admit him quickly! Be no loiterer,
    But come and make me brave for his receiving.

But no one else! – not friends or nearest kin!
    Though an Olympian God should seek me, leaving
    His Heaven, shut fast the door! Don't let him in!

TRANSLATED BY CURTIS HIDDEN PAGE

READING THE BOOK OF HILLS AND SEAS

In the month of June the grass grows high
And round my cottage thick-leaved branches sway.
There is not a bird but delights in the place where
    it rests:
And I too – love my thatched cottage.
I have done my ploughing:
I have sown my seed.
Again I have time to sit and read my books.
In the narrow lane there are no deep ruts:
Often my friends' carriages turn back.
In high spirits I pour out my spring wine
And pluck the lettuce growing in my garden.
A gentle rain comes stealing up from the east
And a sweet wind bears it company.
My thoughts float idly over the story of King Chou
My eyes wander over the pictures of Hills and Seas.
At a single glance I survey the whole Universe.
He will never be happy, whom such pleasures fail
    to please!

TRANSLATED BY ARTHUR WALEY

HOW TO READ A BOOK

When you are reading, and you come to a thorn,
pull it out. Use your knowledge
to heal the book. Don't meddle with poets
who make a living out of finding fault.
They're bad news.

54   MUDDUPALANI
     TRANSLATED BY VELCHERU NARAYANA RAO
     AND DAVID SHULMAN

From BOOK LOVER

I keep collecting books I know
I'll never, never read;
My wife and daughter tell me so,
And yet I never heed.
'Please make me,' says some wistful tome,
'A wee bit of yourself.'
And so I take my treasure home,
And tuck it in a shelf.

And now my very shelves complain;
They jam and over-spill.
They say: 'Why don't you ease our strain?'
'Some day,' I say, 'I will.'
So book by book they plead and sigh;
I pick and dip and scan;
Then put them back, distrest that I
Am such a busy man.

THE ANGEL HANDED ME A BOOK

Placing a book in my hands, the angel said, 'It holds all you would wish to know.' And he vanished.

So I opened the book, which wasn't thick.

It was written in an unknown alphabet.

Scholars translated it, but produced very different versions.

They disagreed even about their own readings, agreeing neither upon the tops or bottoms of them, nor the beginnings, nor the ends.

Toward the close of this vision, it seemed to me that the book melted, until it could not longer be told apart from the world that surrounds us.

      TRANSLATED BY CAROLYN FORCHÉ

FATHER IN THE LIBRARY
From *The World*

A high forehead, and above it tousled hair
On which a ray of sun falls from the window.
And so father wears a bright fluffy crown
When he spreads before him a huge book.

His gown is patterned like that of a wizard.
Softly, he murmurs his incantations.
Only he whom God instructs in magic
Will learn what wonders are hidden in this book.

CZESLAW MILOSZ
TRANSLATED BY THE AUTHOR

TURNING THE PAGE

BOOKS

From the heart of this dark, evacuated campus
I can hear the library humming in the night,
a choir of authors murmuring inside their books
along the unlit, alphabetical shelves,
Giovanni Pontano next to Pope, Dumas next to
    his son,
each one stitched into his own private coat,
together forming a low, gigantic chord of language.

I picture a figure in the act of reading,
shoes on a desk, head tilted into the wind of a book,
a man in two worlds, holding the rope of his tie
as the suicide of lovers saturates a page,
or lighting a cigarette in the middle of a theorem.
He moves from paragraph to paragraph
as if touring a house of endless, paneled rooms.

I hear the voice of my mother reading to me
from a chair facing the bed, books about horses
    and dogs,
and inside her voice lie other distant sounds,
the horrors of a stable ablaze in the night,
a bark that is moving toward the brink of speech

I watch myself building bookshelves in college,
walls within walls, as rain soaks New England,
or standing in a bookstore in a trench coat.

I see all of us reading ourselves away from ourselves,
straining in circles of light to find more light
until the line of words becomes a trail of crumbs
that we follow across a page of fresh snow;
when evening is shadowing the forest
and small birds flutter down to consume the crumbs,
we have to listen hard to hear the voices
of the boy and his sister receding into the woods.

SACRED BOOKS

In the night-study my books converse quietly,
A 1000 tongues so subtle their words slip between
The electron pulse of my nerves and impulse to longing.

The loneliness of books is different than ours
Because we live our lives between the pages.
The book of the white whale does suffice in our
    darkness.

Best that students now don't know the tale
Of Isaac, the cold hike, the Bowie knife
In our beloved father's hand, the lamb

Looking on with affectionate bewilderment.
In a shop window stands a pillar of glued books.
Elegantly shut forever, they bear our sorrows.

We are woven by the winter's tale.
A book beckons us into its house of infinite digression.
A seed suddenly sprung up, swallowing our body,
    our city.

The sacred books have fits of melancholy
Because they have ceased being books, become coins.
Opening a book to the light is to open my wings.

DAVID S. HERRSTROM

THE BOOK AND I

Already I lived in an unmanaged world –
from a book I needed something different.
And along the way it wouldn't hurt,
I kept thinking, if I could please, please,
be enthralled. I put it down –
the merciful language you use
when you've decided the poor dog
would be better off dead. I put the book down
and began to clip the coleus. I made
some long-overdue calls to my relatives,
old attempts at reining in the chaos.
The book remained on the coffee table,
its characters as good as gone, the plod
of their progress now forever curtailed.
They had been sad characters, but in a book
I wanted sadness tuned so it might
give pleasure, I wanted it oddly funny,
or to brilliantly unsettle my heart.
These characters were only sad,
the father cruel but undriven
by any flaws I might share, the son –
like the author – unreliably unreliable.
Some books fail so maddeningly
I've tossed them across the room,
which means they'd been loved

until they broke some big promise,
or forgot one was made.
This book I just wanted to go
quietly, perhaps to some yard sale.
There'd be no afterlife for it, no,
no place for it even on the highest,
out-of-sight shelf in the house.
After all, the others were up there,
my chosens, all spine and substance.

THEY ARRIVED IN TIME

I like to think about writers like James Joyce
Hemingway, Ambrose Bierce, Faulkner, Sherwood
Anderson, Jeffers, D. H. Lawrence, A. Huxley,
John Fante, Gorki, Turgenev, Dostoevsky, Saroyan,
Villon, even Sinclair Lewis, and Hamsun, even
T. S. Eliot and Auden, William Carlos Williams
and Stephen Spender and gutsy Ezra Pound.

they taught me so many things that my parents
never taught me, and
I also like to think of Carson McCullers
with her *Sad Café* and *Golden Eye.*
she too taught me much that my parents
never knew.

I liked to read the hardcover library books
in their simple library bindings
blue and green and brown and light red
I liked the older librarians (male and female)
who stared seriously at one
if you coughed or laughed too loudly,
and even though they looked like my parents
there was no real resemblance.

now I no longer read those authors I once read
with such pleasure,
but it's good to think about them,
and I also
like to look again at photographs of Hart Crane and
Caresse Crosby at Chantilly, 1929
or at photographs of D. H. Lawrence and Frieda
sunning at Le Moulin, 1928.

I like to see André Malraux in his flying outfit
with a kitten on his chest and
I like photos of Artaud in the madhouse
Picasso at the beach with his strong legs
and his hairless head, and then there's
D. H. Lawrence milking that cow
and Aldous at Saltwood Castle, Kent, August
1963.

I like to think about these people
they taught me so many things that I
never dreamed of before.
and they taught me well,
very well
when it was so much needed
they showed me so many things
that I never knew were possible.
those friends

deep in my blood
who
when there was no chance
gave me one.

From INFERNO

'One day, to pass the time away, we read
of Lancelot – how love had overcome him.
We were alone, and we suspected nothing.
    And time and time again that reading led
our eyes to meet, and made our faces pale,
and yet one point alone, defeated us.
    When we had read how the desired smile
was kissed by one who was so true a lover,
this one, who never shall be parted from me,
    while all his body trembled, kissed my mouth.
A Gallehault indeed, that book and he
who wrote it, too; that day we read no more.'
    And while one spirit said these words to me,
the other wept, so that – because of pity –
I fainted, as if I had met my death.
    And then I fell as a dead body falls.

SUPERNATURAL LOVE

My father at the dictionary-stand
Touches the page to fully understand
The lamplit answer, tilting in his hand

His slowly scanning magnifying lens,
A blurry, glistening circle he suspends
Above the word 'Carnation.' Then he bends

So near his eyes are magnified and blurred,
One finger on the miniature word,
As if he touched a single key and heard

A distant, plucked, infinitesimal string,
'The obligation due to every thing
That's smaller than the universe.' I bring

My sewing needle close enough that I
Can watch my father through the needle's eye,
As through a lens ground for a butterfly

Who peers down flower-hallways toward a room
Shadowed and fathomed as this study's gloom
Where, as a scholar bends above a tomb

To read what's buried there, he bends to pore
Over the Latin blossom. I am four,
I spill my pins and needles on the floor

Trying to stitch 'Beloved' X by X.
My dangerous, bright needle's point connects
Myself illiterate to this perfect text

I cannot read. My father puzzles why
It is my habit to identify
Carnations as 'Christ's flowers,' knowing I

Can give no explanation but 'Because.'
Word-roots blossom in speechless messages
The way the thread behind my sampler does

Where following each X I awkward move
My needle through the word whose root is love.
He reads, 'A pink variety of Clove,

Carnatio, the Latin, meaning flesh.'
As if the bud's essential oils brush
Christ's fragrance through the room, the iron-fresh

Odor carnations have floats up to me,
A drifted, secret, bitter ecstasy,
The stems squeak in my scissors, *Child, it's me,*

He turns the page to 'Clove' and reads aloud:
'The clove, a spice, dried from a flower-bud.'
Then twice, as if he hasn't understood,

He reads, 'From French, for *clou*, meaning a nail.'
He gazes, motionless. 'Meaning a nail.'
The incarnation blossoms, flesh and nail,

I twist my threads like stems into a knot
And smooth 'Beloved,' but my needle caught
Within the threads, *Thy blood so dearly bought*,

The needle strikes my finger to the bone.
I lift my hand, it is myself I've sewn,
The flesh laid bare, the threads of blood my own,

I lift my hand in startled agony
And call upon his name, 'Daddy daddy' –
My father's hand touches the injury

As lightly as he touched the page before,
Where incarnation bloomed from roots that bore
The flowers I called Christ's when I was four.

SEPTEMBER EVENING:
DEER AT BIG BASIN

When they talk about angels in books
I think what they mean is this sudden
arrival: this gift of an alien country
we guessed all along,

and how these deer are moving in the dark,
bound to the silence, finding our scent in their way
and making us strange, making us all that we are
in the fall of the light,

as if we had entered the myth
of one who is risen, and one who is left behind
in the gap that remains,

a story that gives us the questions we wanted to ask,
and a sense of our presence as creatures,
about to be touched.

SUNDAY

in an art book
I came across
two paintings by Van Gogh
they hadn't been mounted on banknotes
these two celebrated works
were unremarkable paintings
one was called *Gaugin's Chair*
the other
Van Gogh's Chair
although I didn't go so far
as to buy the book
I was
so moved by what I saw
that I was like
'a chariot driven south
to get north'
and I caught the wrong trolley bus
home

DEAR MARY

Dear Mary,
young Bethlehem girl with torn
blue jeans, you who read your comic books
in a corner among hemp dust and almond trees.
But your comic books are also
our life,
and you can't do anything about it, you
can't change the stories,
it must be like this,
holy Mary: you're dying to
intervene, but you too
are damned to something:
our liberty, your pain.

FLAVIO SANTI
TRANSLATED BY GABRIELE POOLE

THE LIBRARY OF THE BLIND

Entranced, at their tables of mahogany,
Some blind people go over the books like a piano,
The white books that describe
The Braille flowers of remote perfume,
The tactile night that caresses their fingers,
The mane of a colt amidst the rushes.
A scattering of words enters through the hands
And takes a sweet journey to the ear.
Bended over the paper's snow
As if hearing the galloping silence
Or almost looking into the amazement, they caress
      the words
Like a musical instrument.
The evening falls from the other side of the mirror
And in the silent library
The steps of the night bring rumors of legend,
Rumors that reach the book's banks.
Back from the amazement
The words still vibrate in their remembering fingers.

JUAN MANUEL ROCA
TRANSLATED BY RAÚL JAIME GAVIRIA

IN BED WITH A BOOK

In police procedurals they are dying all over town,
the life ripped out of them, by gun, bumper, knife,
hammer, dope, etcetera, and no clues at all.
All through the book the calls come in: body found
in bed, car, street, lake, park, garage, library,
and someone goes out to look and write it down.
Death begins life's whole routine to-do
in these stories of our fellow citizens.

Nobody saw it happen, or everyone saw,
but can't remember the car. What difference does
    it make
when the child will never fall in love, the girl
    will never
have a child, the man will never see a grandchild,
    the old maid
will never have another cup of hot cocoa at bedtime?
Like life, the dead are dead, their consciousness,
as dear to them as mine to me, snuffed out.
What has mind to do with this, when the earth is
    bereaved?

I lie, with my dear ones, holding a fictive umbrella,
while around us falls the real and acid rain.
The handle grows heavier and heavier in my hand.

Unlike life, tomorrow night under the bedlamp
by a quick link of thought someone will find out why,
and the policemen and their wives and I will feel
    better.
But all that's toward the end of the book. Meantime,
    tonight,
without a clue I enter sleep's little rehearsal.

MY BOOKS

Ah, at the thought of my books
I feel like I'm being strangled.
The books I had devotedly collected
since I was 15 or 16.

They'd been my companions for much longer than my
       better half.
Though I had never counted,
there were well over 3000 of them.
Or possibly 4000!

On the morning of June 5th in 1945,
I had them all with me
and witnessed their end
as they all vanished in smoke.

Later I found a place to live.
Someone gave us mattresses.
But my books
my unfortunate books would not come back.

My terribly bleak and desolate life.
O my books.
I turn their pages from time to time in my dreams,
there are some passages I've learned by heart.

IKU TAKENAKA   79
TRANSLATED BY YASUHIRO YOTSUMOTO

IN A SECONDHAND BOOKSHOP

Here's his signature, W. S. Graham,
in tidy pencil inside a first edition
of *Alanna Autumnal* by George Barker.
And he's written the date, August
1944. And the place, Cornwall.
Back then he was twenty-five, at war
with the war, living in a caravan
near Sydney Cove. Picture him there,
sprawled on a cramped bench bed,
feet up against the caravan window
as he pulls this book back on its hinges
and reads, lifting his eyes only occasionally
to the scraps of cloud above Pengersick Lane,
until the clouds become stars,
until he moves into that next world,
beyond Cornwall and beyond books,
of dreams. Did it have, the caravan,
man-made light? Don't tell me
it wasn't the sun and then the moon
that lit his way from word to word
down Barker's trail of young sentences.
Maybe I buy the book in the brief belief
that thoughts can be reciprocal
and travel back and forth through time.
Maybe I want to feel his hand under

my own hand as I turn the old pages and read
We have nothing left for us to do but sicken
at the magnificence of our predecessors.

POETRY READING

Silence falls over the hall; I hatch in the spotlight.

Dancers' legs inside mine restrain their pirouettes,
the unbelievable soprano in my chest
threatens to burst forth and shatter the large glass
    windows
but I don't budge.

The poetry fascist raises my hands to orate something
    overwhelming
about the race of bards
and the entertainer inside me
wants to amuse
until you poke your elbows into each other's ribs
bursting with laughter like comrades-in-comedy
but I don't budge.

I freeze at the microphone scarecrow
leaning over my pages
and read into the darkness quickly
the words I thought of so slowly.

VERY RARELY

He's an old man. Worn out and stooped,
crippled by years, and by excess,
stepping slowly, he moves along the alleyway.
But when he goes inside his house to hide
his pitiful state, and his old age, he considers
the share that he – *he* – still has in youth.

Youths recite his verses now.
His visions pass before their animated eyes.
Their healthy, sensuous minds,
their well-limned, solid flesh,
stir to his own expression of the beautiful.

C. P. CAVAFY   83
TRANSLATED BY DAVID MENDELSOHN

'THIS PAGE IS A CLOUD'

This page is a cloud between whose fraying edges
a headland with mountains appears brokenly
then is hidden again until what emerges
from the now cloudless blue is the grooved sea
and the whole self-naming island, its ochre verges,
its shadow-plunged valleys and a coiled road
threading the fishing villages, the white, silent surges
of combers along the coast, where a line of gulls has
    arrowed
into the widening harbour of a town with no noise,
its streets growing closer like print you can now read,
two cruise ships, schooners, a tug, ancestral canoes,
as a cloud slowly covers the page and it goes
white again and the book comes to a close.

THE GIRL WHO ATE BOOKS

It started with hymn books. In school assembly
she would lick her favourite page, 'Jerusalem the Golden':
sleek and translucent, milk and honey.
The teacher said it was unhygienic.
Besides, he said, this was India paper, a gift of God,
making bibles and hymn books light enough for
    missionaries
to carry into all the dark corners of the world.

But it didn't stop there. Soon she was eating holes
in *Elidor, Little House on the Prairie, Stig of the Dump*.
She still gets hungry in bookshops, recalling the juice
and the grain of it. She grew insatiable, even for thicker,
rough-cut stuff. She would chew on *Real Life Maths*
or *People and Places*, then spit out grey pellets
fit only for flicking at boys' necks.

The teacher sighed and said she should have more
    respect.
He said that a thousand years before paper came to
    England
the Chinese made it from bark and fishing nets.
He said that medieval monks wrote on the soft white
    skins
of stillborn calves, and how would she like to eat that?

FOR MY WIFE, READING IN BED

I know we're living through all the dark we can
     afford.
Thank goodness, then, for this moment's light

and you, holding the night at bay – a hint of frown,
those focused hands, that open book.

I'll match your inward quiet, breath for breath.
What else do we have but words and their absences

to bind and unfasten the knotwork of the heart;
to remind us how mutual and alone we are, how tiny

and significant? Whatever it is you are reading now
my love, read on. Our lives depend on it.

DISCOVERING
READING

THINGS YOU DIDN'T PUT ON
YOUR RÉSUMÉ

How often you got up in the middle of the night
when one of your children had a bad dream,

and sometimes you woke because you thought
you heard a cry but they were all sleeping,

so you stood in the moonlight just listening
to their breathing, and you didn't mention

that you were an expert at putting toothpaste
on tiny toothbrushes and bending down to wiggle

the toothbrush ten times on each tooth while
you sang the words to songs from *Annie*, and

who would suspect that you know the fingerings
to the songs in the first four books of the Suzuki

Violin Method and that you can do the voices
of Pooh and Piglet especially well, though

your absolute favorite thing to read out loud is
Bedtime for Frances and that you picked

up your way of reading it from Glynis Johns,
and it is, now that you think of it, rather impressive

that you read all of Narnia and all of the Ring Trilogy
(and others too many to mention here) to them

before they went to bed and on the way out to
Yellowstone, which is another thing you don't put

on the résumé: how you took them to the ocean
and the mountains and brought them safely home.

WAITING FOR MY FATHER TO PICK ME UP AT THE LIBRARY

In the book I started to read when I came into
    English,
a girl drank from a little bottle labeled, DRINK ME,
and shrank so small, she could fit through a tiny door
into a beautiful garden; but she got scared,
and after a good cry, she ate a cake
marked, EAT ME, and grew too big for the door,
not that she wanted to open it anymore.

It had begun to snow. I was ten, waiting
for my father to pick me up at the library.
I took the book back to the desk. *All done?*
the librarian asked. I'd just checked it out.
The book was an English classic she was sure
a girl like me would like. (Surely, she knew
with her snowy face and magnified eyes

what a girl like me would like.) I told her
I'd already read it. What I meant was I'd already
come through that door and couldn't go back.
But I wasn't about to cry and drown in a pool of tears.
I wasn't about to explain, surrounded by shelves
upon shelves of books she had surely read
why a girl like me was afraid of a storybook.

Soon she would see for herself when he came
through the door that my father had shrunk
since arriving in this country, nothing drastic at first,
but something a kid used to craning her neck
to glimpse his distant face, the sun blinding
her eyes, would surely notice. Stepping out
of that Pan Am flight, he must have sensed how

the scale was shifting, the buildings growing taller,
and the little girl looking up, trying
to gauge what to make of this oversized world
from the look on his face seemed to be
growing older as they disembarked.
How could I have outgrown him, like a toy
I didn't yet have the heart to throw away?

In his Panama hat, his salmon three-piece suit,
with his thick mustache, his swarthy olive skin,
he looked like one of those national-costume dolls
our island tías kept in a cabinet.
This was the trade-off for coming to America:
you became as small as the country you came from,
a speck on an ocean I could blot out with my thumb.

But think of the opportunities for his children!
Here, doors would open with study and application,
which would've been closed to girls like me back
    home.
It was why he had dropped me off at the library
while he went looking for work, why I was
determined to read every book on those shelves.
Until looking up at those towering stacks,

I began scaling back my ambition,
wanting to fit in, hoping he wouldn't come
in the door and embarrass me,
a girl on the lookout at the public library,
waiting to blot him out with a lifted hand
he'd mistake for a wave of hello as I hurried out
pretending to spare him the trouble of coming in —

or so I hope in the retrospect of memory,
watching him grow ever smaller, a trickle of dust
funneling down the hourglass into nothing.

ON LEARNING A SACRED
LANGUAGE IN CHILDHOOD

What you remember:
a verb, and how it
collided with a crow
alighting on the tree
behind your mother's head;

a noun, and how it
spilled off the spoon
falling from
your brother's mouth;

a sentence, and its chill
like the chill
of your teacher's hand
on your shoulder.

Now you keep the books
near your body.
They curl and cry
and will not let you
forget their embrace;
their nouns and verbs
break open your silence.

Their sentences nag
like children
wanting a drink.

You try to quiet them,
but they refuse –
the hopes
and disturbances
of your wizened sleep.

From *ALICE'S ADVENTURES IN WONDERLAND*

'And what is the use of a book,' thought Alice, 'without pictures or conversation?'

THE WORLD BOOK

When the woman in blue serge
held up the sun, my mother
opened the storm door, taking
the whole volume of S
into her hands. The sun
shown as a sun should,
and we sat down at the table
leafing through silks and ships,
saints and subtraction. We passed
Scotland and Spain, street-
cars and seeds and even
the Seven Wonders until
the woman who owned them skipped
to the solar system and said
it could be ours. My mother
thought, as I held my breath,
and while she was writing the check
for everything, A through Z,
I noticed the room with its stove
and saucers and spoons. I was wearing
a sweater and skirt and shoes
and there at the window the sun
was almost as clear as it was
in the diagram where its sunspots,
ninety-three million miles

from the earth and only a page
from Sumatra, were swirling. The woman
stood up, slamming it shut,
and drove down the street to leave us
in Saginaw, where I would wait
for the world to arrive. And each morning,
walking to school, I believed
in the day it would come, when we'd study
Sweden or stars and I'd stand
at the head of the classroom and take
the words of the world from my satchel,
explaining the secrets.

TULA

Books are door-shaped
portals
carrying me
across oceans
and centuries,
helping me feel
less alone.

But my mother believes
that girls who read too much
are unladylike
and ugly,
so my father's books are locked
in a clear glass cabinet. I gaze
at enticing covers
and mysterious titles,
but I am rarely permitted
to touch
the enchantment
of words.

Poems.
Stories.
Plays.
All are forbidden.

Girls are not supposed to think,
but as soon as my eager mind
begins to race, free thoughts
rush in
to replace
the trapped ones.

I imagine distant times
and faraway places.
Ghosts.
Vampires.
Ancient warriors.
Fantasy moves into
the tangled maze
of lonely confusion.

Secretly, I open
an invisible book in my mind,
and I step
through its magical door-shape
into a universe
of dangerous villains
and breathtaking heroes.

Many of the heroes are men
and boys, but some are girls
so tall
strong
and clever
that they rescue other children
from monsters.

CELEBRATING
INDIVIDUAL BOOKS
AND AUTHORS

ON MR. MILTON'S *PARADISE LOST*

When I behold the Poet blind, yet bold,
In slender Book his vast Design unfold,
Messiah Crown'd, *Gods* Reconcil'd Decree,
Rebelling *Angels*, the Forbidden Tree,
Heav'n, Hell, Earth, Chaos, All; the Argument
Held me a while, misdoubting his Intent,
That he would ruine (for I saw him strong)
The sacred Truths to Fable and old Song,
(So *Sampson* groap'd the Temples Posts in spight)
The World o'rewhelming to revenge his Sight.

Yet as I read, soon growing less severe,
I lik'd his Project, the success did fear;
Through that wide Field how he his way should find
O're which lame Faith leads Understanding blind;
Lest he perplext the things he would explain,
And what was easie he should render vain.

Or if a Work so infinite he spann'd,
Jealous I was that some less skilful hand
(Such as disquiet alwayes what is well,
And by ill imitating would excell)
Might hence presume the whole Creations day
To change in Scenes, and show it in a Play.

Pardon me, *mighty Poet*, nor despise
My causeless, yet not impious, surmise.
But I am now convinc'd and none will dare

Within thy Labours to pretend a Share.
Thou hast not miss'd one thought that could be fit,
And all that was improper dost omit:
So that no room is here for Writers left,
But to detect their Ignorance or Theft.

That Majesty which through thy Work doth Reign
Draws the Devout, deterring the Profane.
And things divine thou treatst of in such state
As them preserves, and Thee, inviolate.
At once delight and horrour on us seize,
Thou singst with so much gravity and ease;
And above humane flight dost soar aloft,
With Plume so strong, so equal, and so soft.
The *Bird* nam'd from that *Paradise* you sing
So never Flags, but alwaies keeps on Wing.

Where couldst thou Words of such a compass find?
Whence furnish such a vast expense of Mind?
Just Heav'n Thee, like *Tiresias*, to requite,
Rewards with *Prophesie* thy loss of Sight.

Well might thou scorn thy Readers to allure
With tinkling Rhime, of thy own Sense secure;
While the *Town-Bays* writes all the while and spells,
And like a Pack-Horse tires without his Bells.
Their Fancies like our bushy Points appear,
The Poets tag them; we for fashion wear.
I, too, transported by the *Mode* offend,
And while I meant to *Praise* thee, must Commend.

Thy verse created like thy *Theme* sublime,
In Number, Weight, and Measure, needs not *Rhime*.

ON FIRST LOOKING INTO
CHAPMAN'S HOMER

Much have I travell'd in the realms of gold,
   And many goodly states and kingdoms seen;
   Round many western islands have I been
Which bards in fealty to Apollo hold.
Oft of one wide expanse had I been told,
   That deep-brow'd Homer ruled as his demesne:
   Yet did I never breathe its pure serene
Till I heard Chapman speak out loud and bold:
Then felt I like some watcher of the skies
   When a new planet swims into his ken;
Or like stout Cortez when with eagle eyes
   He stared at the Pacific – and all his men
Look'd at each other with a wild surmise –
   Silent, upon a peak in Darien.

MONTAIGNE

Outside his library window he could see
A gentle landscape terrified of grammar,
Cities where lisping was compulsory,
And provinces where it was death to stammer.

The hefty lay exhausted. O it took
This donnish undersexed conservative
To start a revolution, and to give
The Flesh its weapons to defeat the Book.

When devils drive the reasonable wild,
They strip their adult century so bare,
Love must be regrown from the sensual child.

To doubt becomes a way of definition,
Even belles lettres legitimate as prayer,
And laziness an act of pure contrition.

GEORGE CHAPMAN – THE ILIAD

The football rush of him, and that country knowledge,
That pluck driving through work, endless that
    wearying courage,
Still unwearying. Still face on: and the wide heaven
    taking
At one glance in at his eye: O that set on shaking
Keats, and new wonder brought fresh from mortal
    power.
That first hand still, and in sad heart-break hour
The voice of David brought once again to say
What joy what grief on Man Time's heavy hand
    doth lay.
Homer's rebringer, and of joy that great map-man,
Friend of great makers; scholar, mixed-minded doer,
    George Chapman.

HENRY JAMES

It was the eloquence of the unsaid
thing, the nobility of the deed
not performed. They looked sideways
into each other's eyes, met casually
by intention. It was the significance
of an absence, the deprecation
of what was there, the failure
to prove anything that proved his point.

Richness is in the ability
of poverty to conceal itself.
After the curtains deliberately
kept drawn, his phrases were servants moving
silently about the great house of his prose
letting in sunlight into the empty rooms.

ON ACQUIRING AN ENCYCLOPEDIA

Here's the huge Brockhaus encyclopedia,
with those many crammed volumes and an atlas,
here is Germanic dedication,
here are neo-Platonists and Gnostics,
the first Adam is here and the Adam of Bremen,
the tiger and the Tartar,
painstaking typography and the blue of oceans,
here are time's memory and time's labyrinths,
here are error and truth,
here the protracted miscellany more learned than
     any man,
here the sum total of all late hours kept.
Here, too, are eyes of no use, hands that lose
     their way,
pages unreadable,
the dim semishade of blindness, walls that recede.
But also here is a habit new
to that long-standing habit, the house,
a drawing-card and a presence,
the mysterious love of things –
things unaware of themselves and of us.

     TRANSLATED BY ALAN S. TRUEBLOOD

CANTICO DEL SOLE

The thought of what America would be like
If the Classics had a wide circulation
      Troubles my sleep,
The thought of what America,
The thought of what America,
The thought of what America would be like
If the Classics had a wide circulation
      Troubles my sleep.
Nunc dimittis, now lettest thou thy servant,
Now lettest thou thy servant
      Depart in peace.
The thought of what America,
The thought of what America,
The thought of what America would be like
If the Classics had a wide circulation . . .
      Oh well!
      It troubles my sleep.

WINTER PAGES

So much can be heard
in the stillness
of the snow-swept slopes
of an open book

A train laboring its way across
the Siberian hinterland as trees
hold out napkins of snow to
Zhivago and his fellow passengers

The wind lashing the Overlook Hotel
high in the Colorado Rockies
as a limping man chases small foot-
prints in the drifting snow

Carols warming the Christmas Eve
night in Godric's Hollow as
Harry and Hermione brush snow
off tombstones in the church yard

Where a spring thaw may be just a
page-turn away

TO AN EIGHTEENTH CENTURY POET

Old friend (for such you have lately grown to be
Since your tranquillities have tuned with mine),
Sitting alone, your poems on my knee,
In hours of contemplative candleshine,
I sometimes think your ghost revisits me
And lives upon my lips from line to line.

Dead though you are, the quiet-toned persistence
Of what you tell me with your sober skill
Reminds me how terrestrial existence
Plays tricks with death, and, unextinguished still,
Turns home in loveliest hauntings from the distance
Of antiquated years and works its will.

This is the power, the privilege, the pride
And rich morality of those who write
That hearts may be their highway. They shall ride
Conquering uncharted countries with the bright
Rewards of what they wrought in living light . . .
Who then shall dare to say that they have died?

From ELEGY FOR JOHN DONNE

John Donne has sunk in sleep. His verses sleep.
His images, his rhymes, and his strong lines
fade out of view. Anxiety and sin,
alike grown slack, rest in his syllables.
And each verse whispers to its next of kin,
'Move on a bit.' But each stands so remote
from Heaven's Gates, so poor, so pure and dense,
that all seem one. All are asleep. The vault
austere of iambs soars in sleep. Like guards,
the trochees stand and nod to left and right.
The vision of Lethean waters sleeps.
The poet's fame sleeps soundly at its side.
All trials, all sufferings, are sunk in sleep.
And vices sleep. Good lies in Evil's arms.
The prophets sleep. The bleaching snow seeks out,
through endless space, the last unwhitened spot.
All things have lapsed in sleep. The swarms of books,
the streams of words, cloaked in oblivion's ice,
sleep soundly. Every speech, each speech's truth,
is sleeping. Linked chains, sleeping, scarcely clank.
All soundly sleep: the saints, the Devil, God.
Their wicked servants. Children. Friends. The snow
alone sifts, rustling, on the darkened roads.
And there are no more sounds in the whole world.

116   JOSEPH BRODSKY
      TRANSLATED BY GEORGE L. KLINE

BOCCACCIO SENDS PETRARCH
A COPY OF DANTE

Sure ornament of Italy, whose temples
The Roman leaders crowned, receive this work
Which pleases learned men, amazes common,
Its like composed in no prior age.
The verses of an exiled, uncrowned poet,
Resounding merely in his native tongue –
Let them not rouse your scorn. An unjust fortune
Had caused his exile; for the rest, he wished
To show posterity what modern verse could do.
This was his reason – though often savage men,
Raging with envy, have said that Dante did this
From utter ignorance. Perhaps you know
His studies drew him to the snowy heights,
Through nature's secret spots and hiding places,
And through the ways of heaven and earth and sea,
Aonian founts, Parnassus' peaks and caves,
To Julian Paris and the tardy Briton.
Hence virtue gave him the illustrious name
Of poet, theologian, and philosopher.
And he was almost made another glory
Of Florence; but a cruel, too hasty death
Forbade the laurel crown that he deserved.
If at first sight you think his Muse quite bare,
Unlock with all your mind the bar of Pluto,

The mount and throne of Jove, and you will see
His sense sublime is clothed with sacred shades,
And that on Nysa's peak the Muses move
God's lyre, and all things in a wondrous order
Are drawn. Gladly you'll say: 'Another, Dante,
Will spring in time from him you praise and cherish,
Whom Florence, the great mother of poets, has borne
And now reveres, rejoicing; her son's name
Makes her name great among the world's great cities.'
I pray you now, dear friend, our only hope,
Although your genius penetrates the sky
And though your name extends quite to the stars,
Receive, read through, and cherish and approve
Your fellow citizen, learned and a poet:
You'll do yourself, and win yourself, much favor.
Farewell, the City's glory and the world's.

TRANSLATED BY DAVID THOMPSON

RE-READING JANE

To women in contemporary voice and dislocation
she is closely invisible, almost an annoyance.
Why do we turn to her sampler squares for solace?
Nothing she saw was free of snobbery or class.
Yet the needlework of those needle eyes . . .
We are pricked to tears by the justice of her violence:
Emma on Box Hill, rude to poor Miss Bates,
by Mr Knightley's *were she your equal in situation –*
but consider how far this is from being the case
shamed into compassion, and in shame a grace.

Or wicked Wickham and selfish pretty Willoughby,
their vice pure avarice which, displacing love,
defiled the honour marriages should be made of.
She punished them with very silly wives.
Novels of manners? Hymeneal theology!
Six little circles of hell, with attendant humours.
For what do we live but to make sport for our neighbours
And laugh at them in our turn? The philosophy
paused at the door of Mr Bennet's century;
The Garden of Eden's still there in the grounds of
    Pemberley.

The amazing epitaph's 'benevolence of heart'
precedes 'the extraordinary endowments of her mind'
and would have pleased her, who was not unkind.
Dear votary of order, sense, clear art
and irresistible fun, please pitch our lives
outside self-pity we have wrapped them in
and show us how absurd we'd look to you.
You knew the mischief poetry could do.
Yet when Anne Elliot spoke of *its misfortune*
to be seldom safely enjoyed by those who
enjoy it completely, she spoke for you.

MY FATHER'S SHAKESPEARE

My father must have bought it second-hand,
Inscribed 'To R. S. Elwyn' – who was he?
Published 1890, leather-bound,
In 1961 passed on to me.
November 6th. How old was I? Sixteen.
Doing A level in English Lit.,
In love with Keats and getting very keen
On William Shakespeare. I was thrilled with it,
This gift, glad then, as now, to think
I had been chosen as the keeper of
My father's Shakespeare, where, in dark blue ink,
He wrote, 'To Wendy Mary Cope. With love.'
Love on a page, surviving death and time.
He didn't even have to make it rhyme.

BECAUSE OF
LIBRARIES

DON'T GO INTO THE LIBRARY

The library is dangerous –
Don't go in. If you do

You know what will happen.
It's like a pet store or a bakery –

Every single time you'll come out of there
Holding something in your arms.

Those novels with their big eyes and wagging tails.
Those no-nonsense, all-muscle Dobermans,

All nonfiction and business,
Cuddly when they're young,

But then the first page is turned and no turning back.
And those sleek, fast, beautiful greyhounds: poems.

The doughnut scent of it all, *knowledge*,
The aroma of coffee being made

In all those books, something for everyone,
The deli offerings of civilization itself.

The library is the book of books,
Its concrete and wood and glass covers

Keeping within them the very big,
Very long story of everything.

The library is dangerous, full
Of answers. If you go inside,

You may not come out
The same person who went in.

From FOR THE DEDICATION OF THE
NEW CITY LIBRARY, BOSTON
November 26, 1888

Let in the light! from every age
  Some gleams of garnered wisdom pour,
And, fixed on thought's electric page,
  Wait all their radiance to restore.

Let in the light! in diamond mines
  Their gems invite the hand that delves;
So learning's treasured jewels shine
  Ranged on the alcove's ordered shelves.

From history's scroll the splendor streams,
  From science leaps the living ray;
Flashed from the poet's glowing dreams
  The opal fires of fancy play.

Let in the light! these windowed walls
  Shall brook no shadowing colonnades,
But day shall flood the silent halls
  Till o'er yon hills the sunset fades.

Behind the ever open gate
  No pikes shall fence a crumbling throne,
No lackeys cringe, no courtiers wait, –
  This palace is the people's own!

OLIVER WENDELL HOLMES

'BOOKS ARE DELIGHTFUL SOCIETY'

And now I commend you again to your books. Books are delightful society. If you go into a room and find it full of books – and without even taking them down from their shelves – they seem to speak to you, to bid you welcome.

RANDOM
for Robyn Marsack

*on the occasion of the re-opening of the Scottish Poetry
    Library, 28 October 2015*

Go take a book down from the shelf and open it.
Listen, this isn't 'book' but box,
box full of sound you lift the lid on opening.

Yes, open any item in this place and you'll release
some specific human noise and voice and
song that doesn't need a tune to all-the-truer sing.
Pick one. Pick anything.
Slim volume or expansive, all-inclusive, fat anthology –
neither's a dumb tome of texts to tease mere 'meaning'
        from.
The song's the thing.

And the beauty is, it does away with time, and makes
        it meaningless.
When – this is random, but, say, you flick a page,
here's . . . oh, Ben Jonson
and one man's singular, centuries-old, grief *On my
        First Son –*
here doth lie, said he,
his best piece of poetrie –

so chimes and rhymes with that here-and-now sorrow
      of your very own
that, hurt by his and stung to tears,
you're somehow almost comforted
because he had the guts to tell it terrible and true.

Love and the other stuff? Well, poets do this too.
Listen, this library-silence thrums
with lyric, epic, L=A=N=G=U=A=G=E, Lallans,
loud hip-hop or rap, maybe the Metaphysicals,
the Silver, Black Mountain, the Beats
and all the big-stuff always – Shakespeare's sonnets,
oor ain bard Burns (*chiefly in the Scots dialect*), Gaelic's
      òran mór.
Here's the murmur of the Modernists,
the auld breath-and-beat of the balladeer –
oh, and – a word in your ear –
they've got a lot of her, thank God, so – *hypocrite*
      lecteur,
ton semblable, ta soeur et ton frère –
dae mind *Anon.*
She's aye been baith *the real McCoy*
and your perfect contemporary.
All that. And yet it's not cacophony.

Go in. Pick up a book. Enjoy.

LIBRARY

we search for the most esoteric knowledge
climb ladders to reach the highest sections in the
    stacks
rummage through the shelves with spiders
raising clouds of dust
that hover near the ceiling
we hold our breath and
barely keep our balance
like aerialists
as we dive into the thickest tomes
without the slightest hope of ever emerging
books swallow us up like the sea
we grab onto carved overhangs
and somehow manage to stay afloat
then when we lose our strength
breathless and covered with plaster
we seem to find
in the thicket of leather bindings and hard-covers
pressed against the wall
the small warm
nest
of a simple swallow

YURI ANDRUKHOVYCH   131
TRANSLATED BY VIRLANA TKACZ AND
WANDA PHIPPS

LIBRARY

In this mausoleum of words
every page guards
an uncertain memory,
a dusty immortality

Sometimes
in hours unpredictable
a stranger leafs slowly through the emptiness
and from the bottom of the pages
a frozen music
starts crackling

ON THE SIXTH FLOOR
(Mažvydas Library)

An elevator, murmuring quietly,
Lifts us into a sky of books.
Eyes closed, you twist your hair around your finger:
Slumber is a soft and warm cocoon.
It will tear, when you step into the labyrinth of
    shelves.
When you hang your I.D. around your neck.

In the nearby prison's yellow cages, they read the
    script
Another way, with the whole body. On Iron Wolf
    Street
The cars race, competing toward success.
Here only twilight, hours on end, twilight . . .
At lunch you'll drink juice from a wine glass.
The pungence sticking to the corner of your lips.

You'll wander down the aisles, not even searching
For the beginning or end of the letters.
As if saying goodbye, you'll touch the spines of the
    books.
For you know, how one waits for a sign. Just a
    stirring.

How on understanding, everything shines.
How the shelves are endless.

The door opens onto the dim corridor.
But my electricity
Has grazed your hair.
Not moving, not paying any attention,
You stand and drink your image,
Which duplicates itself in the elevator's mirrors.

TRANSLATED BY KERRY SHAWN KEYS

ELEGY

Not every day but most days that summer

I went calmly and quietly and climbed

to the sixth floor of the library and walked

not fast and not slow but with purpose

down the last row and reached

almost without looking to the same

place on the shelf and pulled out

the large book and carried it to a chair

that looks out toward the ridge, to a mountain

that is there, whether it is or it isn't,

the mountain people love, maybe for this,

love and die with all their love,

trying, and I opened to the page

where I left off before, and sometimes the library

announced it was closing, sometimes I got hungry,

sometimes it looked like rain, and I'd close the book

and carry it again, with purpose, back to its exact

place on the shelf, and I'd walk down the stairs

and out of the building, and it was like

I'd left it ticking.

LIBRARY

Amidst the sweets and
Dust of the stacks
I edge from book to book like a grimy kid,
Flattening his nose against an infinitude
Of candy store and bake shop fronts.
Always I get whiffs of things *delicioso*.
It's as sensual as that, and as lonesome;
And alienating. I'm edging round
A lethe pool, sometimes with one numb toe in,
And half inclined to hold my nose and jump.
It is so mirror-clear and parsley fresh.

Quickly, look up something about My Lai
Or Dachau, or plain New York. The hurt
Will keep you present and alert
For decent citizenship.

ROBERT L. CHAPMAN   137

LIBRARY

In the silence of the night when the living have left,
the whispers begin.

Penelope and Odysseus continue their yearning
    conversation
from the night they were reunited. Stalin and Hitler
    volley
insults across aisles, Sisyphus's bride bemoans
    hitching her life
to an old workaholic bugger.

Barbara Cartland is pushed up against Casanova,
Mahler is making moves on Moby.

On the children's floor, a skipping of rhymes,
huffing of wolves and frantic flight of fairies.

The books smell of Russia, of wood, of wet leaves.
They hold crayon scribblings, lost letters,
exclamations and whoops of marginalia.

In the basement at the bottom of the book chute
the Koran hurtles down and rests on the Bible.
The holy sing together.

As morning sun fingers across the shelves
the books are stilled, waiting like abandoned dogs
for the warmth of hands on their spines.

BECAUSE OF LIBRARIES WE CAN
SAY THESE THINGS

She is holding the book close to her body,
carrying it home on the cracked sidewalk,
down the tangled hill.
If a dog runs at her again,
she will use the book as a shield.

She looked hard among the long lines
of books to find this one.
When they start talking about money,
when the day contains such long and hot places,
she will go inside.
An orange bed is waiting.
Story without corners.
She will have two families.
They will eat at different hours.

She is carrying a book past the fire station
and the five-and-dime.
What this town has not given her
the books will provide; a sheep,
a wilderness of new solutions.
The book has already lived through its troubles.
The book has a calm cover, a straight spine.

When the step returns to itself
as the best place for sitting
and the old men up and down the street
are latching their clippers,
she will not be alone.
She will have a book to open
and open and open.
Her life starts here.

ON THE LIBRARY

it shone at night
it shone beautifully

it shone like the eddystone
it shone like the fire-cave
it shone like the old torpedo works
it shone like honeycomb spreadsheets
it shone like alchemy alley
it shone like aurora midnight mass
it shone like a plainchant surge
it shone like a troubadour fragment
it shone like test-site instruments
it shone like towerblock hypodermics
it shone like a harvest moon supper
it shone like famine eyes
it shone like harmonica railtrack
it shone like the tiger sonata
it shone like chandelier futures
it shone like the twilight home past
it shone like news from another star
it shone like the road to ruin
it shone like iron in the soul
it shone like an ampoule of angel dust
it shone like a fistful of martyr clippings
it shone like oranges in a net

it shone like torches in a deep dark forest
it shone like grandma's fireside
it shone like the wicked queen's smile
it shone like the necklace left in the laurel
it shone like the ring spilled in the reeds
it shone like a god's pursuit sandals
it shone like an autumn arboretum
it shone like the cherry pond spring
it shone like a thief's deep pockets
it shone like a jackdaw's escape velocity
it shone like a pirate's night-sweats
it shone like riot in lakeside towns
it shone like an islay lock-in
it shone like a boxful of butterflies
it shone like a web at the wood's edge
it shone like blazing hilltop victory
it shone like the valley of last resort
it shone like the story of you and me

it shone all night

From AN ODE ADDRESSED TO
MR. JOHN ROUSE,

LIBRARIAN, OF THE UNIVERSITY OF OXFORD,

On a lost Volume of my Poems, which he desired me to re-place, that he might add them to my other Works deposited in the Library.*

[The lost volume was a copy of Milton's *Poemata*, 1645. This Latin ode was written in January 1646 and first appeared in print in 1673. It begins in Latin 'Gemelle cultu simplici gaudens liber'.]

ANTISTROPHE

Say, little book, what furtive hand
Thee from thy fellow-books convey'd,
What time, at the repeated suit
    Of my most learned friend,
I sent thee forth, an honour'd traveller,
From our great city to the source of Thames,
        Cærulean sire!
Where rise the fountains, and the raptures ring,
    Of the Aonian choir,
    Durable as yonder spheres,
    And through the endless lapse of years
      Secure to be admired? . . .

But thou, my book, though thou hast stray'd,
Whether by treach'ry lost,
Or indolent neglect, thy bearer's fault,
From all thy kindred books,
To some dark cell, or cave forlorn,
Where thou endur'st, perhaps,
The chafing of some hard untutor'd hand,
Be comforted –
For lo, again the splendid hope appears
That thou may'st yet escape
The gulfs of Lethe, and on oary wings
Mount to the everlasting courts of Jove!

SHUT NOT YOUR DOORS TO ME, PROUD LIBRARIES

Shut not your doors to me, proud libraries,
For that which was lacking among you all, yet needed
     most, I bring;
A book I have made for your dear sake, O soldiers,
And for you, O soul of man, and you, love of comrades;
The words of my book nothing, the life of it
     everything;
A book separate, not link'd with the rest, nor felt by
     the intellect;
But you will feel every word, O Libertad! arm'd
     Libertad!
It shall pass by the intellect to swim the sea, the air,
With joy with you, O soul of man.

THE MYSTERY OF WORDS

[Here then] is the final mystery as well as the final power of words: that not even across great distances of time and space do they ever lose their capacity for becoming incarnate. And when these words tell of virtue and nobility, when they move us closer to that truth and gentleness of spirit by which we become fully human, the reading of them is sacramental; and a library is as holy a place as any temple is holy because through the words which are treasured in it the Word itself becomes flesh again and again and dwells among us and within us, full of grace and truth.

STEPPING OUT OF POETRY

What would you give for one of the old yellow
    streetcars
rocking toward you again through the thick snow?

What would you give for the feeling of joy as you
    climbed
up the three iron steps and took your place by the cold
    window?

Oh, what would you give to pick up your stack of
    books
and walk down the icy path in front of the library?

What would you give for your dream
to be as clear and simple as it was then
in the dark afternoons, at the old scarred tables?

From ODE. MR. COWLEY'S BOOK
PRESENTING IT SELF TO THE
UNIVERSITY LIBRARY OF OXFORD

Hail Learnings *Pantheon*! Hail the sacred Ark
Where all the World of Science do's imbarque!
Which ever shall withstand, and hast so long
    withstood,
   Insatiate Times devouring Flood.
Hail Tree of Knowledge, thy leaves Fruit! which well
Dost in the midst of Paradise arise,
   Oxford and the Muses Paradise,
From which may never Sword the blest expell.
Hail Bank of all past Ages! where they lye
T'inrich with interest Posterity!
   Hail Wits Illustrious Galaxy!
Where thousand Lights into one brightness spread;
Hail living University of the Dead!

FAME'S LIBRARY WITHIN THE TEMPLE

In Fame's great library are records placed;
What act's not there, into oblivion's cast.
There stand the shelves of time, where books do lie,
Which books are tied by chains of destiny.
The master of this place they Favour call,
Where Care, the door-keeper, doth lock up all,
Yet not so fast, but Brib'ry in doth steal,
Cozenage, Partiality – and truth not reveal.
But bribery through all the world takes place,
And off'rings, as a bribe, in heaven find grace.
Then let not men disdain a bribe to take,
Since gods do blessings give for a bribe's sake.

THE LIBRARY

'Let there be light!' God spake of old,
And over chaos dark and cold,
And through the dead and formless frame
Of nature, life and order came.

Faint was the light at first that shone
On giant fern and mastodon,
On half-formed plant and beast of prey,
And man as rude and wild as they.

Age after age, like waves, o'erran
The earth, uplifting brute and man;
And mind, at length, in symbols dark
Its meanings traced on stone and bark.

On leaf of palm, on sedge-wrought roll,
On plastic clay and leathern scroll,
Man wrote his thoughts; the ages passed,
And lo! the Press was found at last!

Then dead souls woke; the thoughts of men
Whose bones were dust revived again;
The cloister's silence found a tongue,
Old prophets spake, old poets sung.

And here, to-day, the dead look down,
The kings of mind again we crown;
We hear the voices lost so long,
The sage's word, the sibyl's song.

Here Greek and Roman find themselves
Alive along these crowded shelves;
And Shakespeare treads again his stage,
And Chaucer paints anew his age.

As if some Pantheon's marbles broke
Their stony trance, and lived and spoke,
Life thrills along the alcoved hall,
The lords of thought await our call!

IN A CARDIFF ARCADE, 1952

One of those little shops too small
for the worlds they hold, where words
that sing you to sleep, stories
that stalk your dreams,
open like golden windows in a wall.

One small room leads to another,
the first bright-windowed on the street,
alluring, luminous. The other is dusk,
walled with pressed pages, old books
with leathery breath and freckled leaves.

What stays is not the book alone
but where you took it down,
how it felt in your hands,
how she wrapped it in brown paper,
how you carried it home,

how it holds wild seas
that knock the earth apart,
how words burn, freeze,
to break and heal your heart.

GILLIAN CLARKE   153

IN THE ENGLISH FACULTY LIBRARY, OXFORD
(*for R.K.M.*)

It is a house of stairs.   Books strain
Alphabetically upwards.   Critics sprang
To eminence on their pages, and these bowed
Figures muse of vaulting after,
Through duly attested up-gradings
To doctorates.   Beneath the spires
The academics dream.

It is a house of light.   Technology
Illumines the dark reading, the blurred word.
With perfect vision, the bright-haired
(At sea with their sex-lives, finances,
Their futures, their tutors, sentenced
To match next essay with surly text)
Pelt down the feint tracks of dead game.

It is a house of peace.   Gentle-
footed librarians pace the precincts.
Owen's legacy lies quiet.   Sotto voce
Students make assignations and jokes; softly
They sharpen their pencils; inaudibly biros
Utter the last judgment.

It is a charnelhouse.   The untongued dead
Wince at the touch of the lucky living.

It is a charnelhouse.   The quick and young
Choke on the breath of refractory clay.

Down in the cellars the dead men grumble
Resenting, resisting the patterns
We make of their bones.

LITERATURE FOR DESOLATE ISLANDS
From *A Fable for Critics*

I've thought very often 'twould be a good thing
In all public collections of books, if a wing
Were set off by itself, like the seas from the dry lands,
Marked *Literature suited to desolate islands*,
And filled with such books as could never be read
Save by readers of proofs, forced to do it for bread, –
Such books as one's wrecked on in small country
    taverns,
Such as hermits might mortify over in caverns,
Such as Satan, if printing had then been invented,
As the climax of woe, would to Job have presented,
Such as Crusoe might dip in, although there are
    few so
Outrageously cornered by fate as poor Crusoe;

    . . .

I propose to shut up every doer of wrong
With these desperate books, for such term, short
    or long,
As by statute in such cases made and provided,
Shall be by your wise legislators decided.

CLOSING TIME: PUBLIC LIBRARY

At ten o'clock its great gong sounds the dread
Prelude to splendour. I push back my chair,
And all the people leave their books. We flock,
Still acquiescent, down the marble stair
Into the dark where we can't read. And thought
Swoops down insatiate through the starry air.

LESBIA HARFORD   157

ADULT FICTION

I always loved libraries, the quiet of them,
The smell of the plastic covers and the paper
And the tables and the silence of them,
The silence of them that if you listened wasn't silence,
It was the murmur of stories held for years on shelves
And the soft clicking of the date stamp,
The soft clickety-clicking of the date stamp.

I used to go down to our little library on a Friday night
In late summer, just as autumn was thinking about
Turning up, and the light outside would be the colour
Of an Everyman cover and the lights in the library
Would be soft as anything, and I'd sit at a table
And flick through a book and fall in love
With the turning of the leaves, the turning of the
        leaves.

And then at seven o'clock Mrs Dove would say
In a voice that wasn't too loud so it wouldn't
Disturb the books 'Seven o'clock please . . .'
And as I was the only one in the library's late summer
        rooms
I would be the only one to stand up and close my book
And put it back on the shelf with a sound like a kiss,
Back on the shelf with a sound like a kiss.

And I'd go out of the library and Mrs Dove would
    stand
For a moment silhouetted by the Adult Fiction,
And then she would turn the light off and lock the
    door
And go to her little car and drive off into the night
That was slowly turning the colour of ink and I would
    stand
For two minutes and then I'd walk over to the dark
    library
And just stand in front of the dark library.

IAN McMILLAN   159

ALWAYS THE
LIBRARIANS

IF LIBRARIANS WERE HONEST

'. . . a book indeed sometimes debauched me from
my work . . .'
– Benjamin Franklin

If librarians were honest,
they wouldn't smile, or act
welcoming. They would say,
You need to be careful. Here
be monsters. They would say,
These rooms house heathens
and heretics, murderers and
maniacs, the deluded, desperate,
and dissolute. They would say,
These books contain knowledge
of death, desire, and decay,
betrayal, blood, and more blood;
each is a Pandora's box, so why
would you want to open one.
They would post danger
signs warning that contact
might result in mood swings,
severe changes in vision,
and mind-altering effects.

If librarians were honest
they would admit the stacks
can be more seductive and
shocking than porn. After all,
once you've seen a few
breasts, vaginas, and penises,
more is simply more,
a comforting banality,
but the shelves of a library
contain sensational novelties,
a scandalous, permissive mingling
of Malcolm X, Marx, Melville,
Merwin, Millay, Milton, Morrison,
and anyone can check them out,
taking them home or to some corner
where they can be debauched
and impregnated with ideas.

If librarians were honest,
they would say, *No one*
spends time here without being
changed. Maybe you should
go home. While you still can.

ENQUIRY DESK

Do you have the one
with that poem they read at the funeral
in that movie?

Do you have the one
with that poem that they used to make us
learn at secondary school?

Do you have the one
with that poem that the Librarians decided was
too beautiful to catalogue and classify?

Do you have the one
with that poem that knows the difference between
ae hing and *anither hing*?

Do you have the one
with that poem that sat in the corner for ten years and
    then
exploded like a grenade in a crowded space?

Do you have the one
with that poem from the box of love letters
the city keeps under its bed?

165

Do you have the one
with that poem that identifies the chemical properties
of the ghosts of ideas it contains?

Do you have the one
with that poem that is a cache of weapons
which can never be put beyond use?

Do you have the one
with that poem that has learned to impersonate
other poems it has never met?

Do you have the one
with that poem that has mastered chiaroscuro
yet can also emulsion a room in an hour?

Do you have the one
with that poem that stole into my lover's bed
when I wasn't reading it?

Do you have the one
with that poem that is bigger on the inside
that on the outside?

Do you have the one
– you must have it –
with that poem that is a Library in itself,
each leaf a life we might one day live?

I don't know what it's called
but it calls, it calls.

MAPLE VALLEY BRANCH LIBRARY, 1967

For a fifteen-year-old there was plenty
to do: browse the magazines,
slip into the Adult Section to see
what vast *tristesse* was born of rush-hour traffic,
décolletés, and the plague of too much money.
There was so much to discover – how to
lay out a road, the language of flowers,
and the place of women in the tribe of Moost.
There were equations elegant as a French twist,
fractal geometry's unwinding maple leaf;

I could follow, step-by-step, the slow disclosure
of a pineapple Jell-O mold – or take
the path of Harold's purple crayon through
the bedroom window and onto a lavender
spill of stars. Oh, I could walk any aisle
and smell wisdom, put a hand out to touch
the rough curve of bound leather,
the harsh parchment of dreams.

As for the improbable librarian
with her salt and paprika upsweep,
her British accent and sweater clip
(mom of a kid I knew from school) –
I'd go up to her desk and ask for help

on bareback rodeo or binary codes,
phonics, Gestalt theory,
lead poisoning in the Late Roman Empire,
the play of light in Dutch Renaissance painting;
I would claim to be researching
pre-Columbian pottery or Chinese foot-binding,
but all I wanted to know was:
Tell me what you've read that keeps
that half smile afloat
above the collar of your impeccable blouse.

So I read *Gone with the Wind* because
it was big, and haiku because they were small.
I studied history for its rhapsody of dates,
lingered over Cubist art for the way
it showed all sides of a guitar at once.
All the time in the world was there, and sometimes
all the world on a single page.
As much as I could hold
on my plastic card's imprint I took,

greedily: six books, six volumes of bliss,
the stuff we humans are made of:
words and sighs and silence,
ink and whips, Brahma and cosine,
corsets and poetry and blood sugar levels –
I carried it home, five blocks of aluminum siding

and past the old garage where, on its boarded-up
     doors,
someone had scrawled:

I CAN EAT AN ELEPHANT
IF I TAKE SMALL BITES.

Yes, I said to no one in particular: *That's
what I'm gonna do!*

IN THE LIBRARY

In the library the first time
I stood in a pool of awe.
Wonder for taking, acres of promises.
The lady with the specs
And the hair-tuft on her cheek
Asking me if I had washed my hands.
The holy ritual of the water – what was this?
Superstitious as a Goth, I grabbed and ran.
At the bus-stop I discovered I had looted
A book about a girls' school. It was good.

Ridiculous, small moment but it stays.
Seed of an anger perennially mine.
The hope I lugged to that place
Back and forth and afterwards
Brought to how many books . . .
Raising my eyes
From several million pages I have seen
That small boy standing there.

The time it took
The fields there were to cut, the loads to carry,
Hutches to be filled
The roads to lay
The tired nights in narrow beds, the rage

To bring him to his patch of floor,
His eyes like begging bowls.

I don't forgive
The determined absence of himself he was to find.
The self-perpetuating silliness, the cliques
Of convoluted silences, the lies,
The long articulate anathema
Against him and his pals.
They were nowhere to be seen unless those bits
Between the lines and down the edges
Were for them.

No wonder they drew graffiti in the margins.

A POEM FOR MY LIBRARIAN,
MRS. LONG

*(You never know what troubled little girl needs
      a book)*

At a time when there was no tv before 3:00 P.M.
And on Sunday none until 5:00
We sat on front porches watching
The jfg sign go on and off greeting
The neighbors, discussing the political
Situation congratulating the preacher
On his sermon

There was always the radio which brought us
Songs from wlac in nashville and what we would
      now call
Easy listening or smooth jazz but when I listened
Late at night with my portable (that I was so
      proud of)
Tucked under my pillow
I heard nat king cole and matt dennis, june christy
      and ella fitzgerald
And sometimes sarah vaughan sing black coffee
Which I now drink
It was just called music

There was a bookstore uptown on gay street
Which I visited and inhaled that wonderful odor
Of new books
Even today I read hardcover as a preference paperback
    only
As a last resort

And up the hill on vine street
(The main black corridor) sat our carnegie library
Mrs. Long always glad to see you
The stereoscope always ready to show you faraway
Places to dream about

Mrs. Long asking what are you looking for today
When I wanted *Leaves of Grass* or alfred north
    whitehead
She would go to the big library uptown and I now
    know
Hat in hand to ask to borrow so that I might borrow

Probably they said something humiliating since
    southern
Whites like to humiliate southern blacks

But she nonetheless brought the books
Back and I held them to my chest
Close to my heart

And happily skipped back to grandmother's house
Where I would sit on the front porch
In a gray glider and dream of a world
Far away

I love the world where I was
I was safe and warm and grandmother gave me neck
    kisses
When I was on my way to bed

But there was a world
Somewhere
Out there
And Mrs. Long opened that wardrobe
But no lions or witches scared me
I went through
Knowing there would be
Spring

THE BEAUTIFUL LIBRARIANS

The beautiful librarians are dead,
The fairly recent graduates who sat
Like Françoise Hardy's shampooed sisters
With cardigans across their shoulders
On quiet evenings at the issue desk,
Stamping books and never looking up
At where I stood in adoration.

Once I glimpsed the staffroom
Where they smoked and (if the novels
Were correct) would speak of men.
I still see the blue Minis they would drive
Back to their flats around the park,
To Blossom Dearie and red wine
Left over from a party I would never

Be a member of. Their rooms looked down
On dimming avenues of lime.
I shared the geography but not the world
It seemed they were establishing
With such unfussy self-possession, nor
The novels they were writing secretly
That somehow turned to 'Mum's old stuff'.

Never to even brush in passing
Yet nonetheless keep faith with them,
The ice queens in their realms of gold –
It passes time that passes anyway.
Book after book I kept my word
Elsewhere, long after they were gone
And all the brilliant stock was sold.

ELEGY

ON THE DEATH OF ESTHER CATERER,
LIBRARIAN OF SURRY-STREET BOOK ROOMS

Ye book worms, a' wi' sorrow meet,
Nor wi' few tears your een be weet;
For ance, spite o' the warld's deceit,
   By pity led,
Be your's the wail o' Surry Street,
   Auld Esther's dead!
She was a canty clattering dame,
A servant gude; abroad, at hame,
She had an honest matron's fame;
   Nor could I spread
A mickle stain owre a' her name –
   Auld Esther's dead!

HEARING OF ALIA MUHAMMED BAKER'S STROKE

How a Basra librarian
could haul the books each night,
load by load, into her car,

the war ticking like a clock
about to wake. Her small house
swimming in them. How, the British

now crossing the limits
of Basra, the neighbors struck
a chain to pass the bags of books

over the wall, into a restaurant,
until she could bring them all,
like sandbags, into her home,

some thirty thousand of them,
before the library, and her brain,
could finally flood into flame.

THE WRITING
OF BOOKS

THE JOY OF WRITING

Where is a written deer running through a written
     forest?
Whether to drink from written water
which will reflect its mouth like a carbon?
Why is it raising its head, does it hear something?
Propped on four legs borrowed from the truth
it pricks up its ears from under my fingers.
Silence – that word, too, is rustling on paper
and parts the branches caused by the word 'forest.'

Over a white page letters are ready to jump
and they may take a bad turn.
Sentences capable of bringing to bay,
and against which there is no help.
In a drop of ink there are quite a few
hunters squinting one eye,
ready to rush down a vertical pen,
to encircle the deer, to take aim.

They forget that this is not life here.
Other laws rule here, in black and white.
An instant will last as long as I desire.
It will allow a division into small eternities
each full of buckshot stopped in its flight.
If I command, nothing here will happen ever.

Not even a leaf will fall without my accord,
or a blade of grass bend under a dot of a hoof.

And so there is such a world
on which I impose an autonomous Fate?
A time which I bind with fetters of signs?
A life that at my command is perpetual?

The joy of writing.
A chance to make things stay.
A revenge of a mortal hand.

ON LEARNING OLD VOCABULARY

Words don't sleep in dictionaries. They hang about
On street corners, aimless, play with munitions,
Like kids that carry war inside even when it's done.
We never would've guessed, Herr Nobel, that
    dynamite
Might make them interchangeable: material, moral, art.
Particles that went flying from that day, articles

In all the scientific journals, thousands per subject –
A desert track of knowledge. And the great gulfs
Between this and that meaning of 'Devotion',
The satellite pictures of 'Delirium' or 'Democracy'.

It's down to him, he destroyed it all, the baby face,
Who breathed in smog and blew it out as gold dust.
It's down to him, who sold the dawn for scrap.
Don't stop the dictation, you poets. Words don't sleep.

VOCATIVE

English is my native

anguish. I was born here,

read here, teased and torn here.

Vocative, ablative,

locative, alive:

English was a dislocation

navigating oceans.

Wherever it arrived,

it broke and brokered words,

its little bits of Britain

pilfered, bartered, written,

looted, hoarded, heard.

Papa swapped a world

for shiny colored beads,

for dandelion seeds.

We are subject verbs.

The root word of my name

hooks a foreign land,

long-since-shifted sand

books cannot reclaim.

Graft of tongue, gift of dust,

mother and stranger, sing

the kedgeree, the everything

at once you've made of us.

From ARS POETICA

The pull of the fish on the line
like the hard steady current of the river

and you pulling back equally steadily
in water to your waist

under a summer sun
that bakes the back of your neck

jigs of splashy light teasing the eye
delighting not distracting you

from the thing you are trying to catch
that is trying to flee

THE TELLER OF TALES

When I'm walking, everything
on earth gets up
and stops me and whispers to me,
and what they tell me is their story.

And the people walking
on the road leave me their stories,
I pick them up where they fell
in cocoons of silken thread.

Stories run through my body
or sit purring in my lap.
So many they take my breath away,
buzzing, boiling, humming.
Uncalled they come to me,
and told, they still won't leave me.

The ones that come down through the trees
weave and unweave themselves,
and knit me up and wind me round
until the sea drives them away.

But the sea that's always telling stories,
the wearier I am the more it tells me . . .

The people who cut trees,
the people who break stones,
want stories before they go to sleep.

Women looking for children
who got lost and don't come home,
women who think they're alive
and don't know they're dead,
every night they ask for stories,
and I return tale for tale.

In the middle of the road, I stand
between rivers that won't let me go,
and the circle keeps closing
and I'm caught in the wheel.

The riverside people tell me
of the drowned woman sunk in grasses
and her gaze tells her story,
and I graft the tales into my open hands.

To the thumb come stories of animals,
to the index fingers, stories of my dead.
There are so many tales of children
they swarm on my palms like ants.

When my arms held
the one I had, the stories
all ran as a blood-gift
in my arms, all through the night.
Now, turned to the East,
I'm giving them away because I forget them.

Old folks want them to be lies.
Children want them to be true.
All of them want to hear my own story,
which, on my living tongue, is dead.

I'm seeking someone who remembers it
leaf by leaf, thread by thread.
I lend her my breath, I give her my legs,
so that hearing it may waken it for me.

GABRIELA MISTRAL   191
TRANSLATED BY URSULA K. LE GUIN

SOUND AND SENSE
From *Essay on Criticism*

True ease in writing comes from art, not chance,
As those move easiest who have learn'd to dance.
'Tis not enough no harshness gives offence,
The sound must seem an Echo to the sense:
Soft is the strain when Zephyr gently blows,
And the smooth stream in smoother numbers flows;
But when loud surges lash the sounding shoar,
The hoarse, rough verse should like the torrent roar.
When Ajax strives, some rock's vast weight to throw,
The line too labours, and the words move slow;
Not so, when swift Camilla scours the plain,
Flies o'er th' unbending corn, and skims along the main.
Hear how Timotheus' vary'd lays surprize,
And bid alternate passions fall and rise!

From *SONGS FROM BELOW*

It's easy to talk, and writing words on the page
doesn't involve much risk as a general rule:
you might as well be knitting late at night
in a warm room, in a soft, treacherous light.
The words are all written in the same ink,
'flower' and 'fear' are nearly the same for example,
and I could scrawl 'blood' the length of the page
without splashing the paper or hurting
myself at all.

After a while it gets you down, this game,
you no longer know what it was you set out to achieve
instead of exposing yourself to life
and doing something useful with your hands.

That's when you can't escape,
when pain is a figure tearing the fog
that shrouds you, striking away
the obstacles one by one, covering
the swiftly decreasing distance, now
so close you can make out nothing
but his mug wider than the sky.

To speak is to lie, or worse: a craven
insult to grief or a waste
of the little time and energy at our disposal.

*

Might there be things which lend themselves
more readily to words, and live with them
– those glad moments gladly found in poems,
light that releases words
as if erasing them; while other things
resist them, change them, destroy them even –

as if language resisted death,
or rather, as if death consumed
even the words?

AUTHOR'S PRAYER

If I speak for the dead, I must leave
this animal of my body,

I must write the same poem over and over
for an empty page is the white flag of their surrender.

If I speak for them, I must walk on the edge
of myself, I must live as a blind man

who runs through rooms without
touching the furniture.

Yes, I live. I can cross the streets asking 'What year
    is it?'
I can dance in my sleep and laugh

in front of the mirror.
Even sleep is a prayer, Lord,

I will praise your madness, and
in a language not mine, speak

of music that wakes us, music
in which we move. For whatever I say

is a kind of petition and the darkest
days must I praise.

From EUROPE: A PROPHECY

'Then tell me what is the material world, and is it
    dead?'
He, laughing answer'd: 'I will write a book on leaves
    of flowers
If you will feed me on love-thoughts & give me now
    and then
A cup of sparkling poetic fancies; so, when I am tipsie,
I'll sing to you to this soft lute, and shew you all alive
The world, where every particle of dust breathes forth
    its joy.'

WILLIAM BLAKE   197

THE PRIVACY OF TYPEWRITERS

I am an old book troglodyte
one who composes on paper
and types up the result
as many times as need be.

The computer scares me,
its crashes and codes,
its links with spies and gunshot,
its text that looks pre-published.

I fear a carriage
that doesn't move or ding,
no inky marching hammers
leaping up and subsiding.

I trust the spoor of botch,
whiteouts where thought deepened,
wise freedom from Spell Check,
sheets to sell the National Library.

I fear the lore
of that baleful misstruck key
that fills a whiskered screen
with a writhe of child pornography

and the doors booting open
and the cops handcuffing me
to a gristlier video culture
coralline in an ever colder sea.

CONFRONTING NUJIANG

The poet stands on the bank of Nujiang River, stands
      at blood-red dusk.
Once again, he must cross.
They say at such moments
heroes will swim it and traitors will swim it too.
Only cowards tremble.

But a bridge has been built over the river.
The epic has been written.
Heroes and traitors have died.
At this blood-red dusk
the poet can be only one of the common passersby.

Look, the poet still stands on the bank of Nujiang River,
still at that blood-red dusk.
The bridge, like a line,
appears suddenly in a poem, lets him swim across.
But what really brings him close to billowing waves
is the metaphor of a waterfowl,

a red-billed waterfowl that dives down to the surface
      of the river,
flits over cold light glittering on great waves,
pierces finally to the countless round stones in the
      dark night of the river bottom.

200   LI SEN
        TRANSLATED BY WANG HO AND
        STEVEN SCHROEDER

A WRITER'S FOUNTAIN PEN TALKING

I gave out one day and left a woman
tied to a railroad track.
                    And what happened next?
The train couldn't go on; it stopped with a
foot in the air, like Napoleon's horse on the bridge
when it knew the plank was gone.
                    What ever happened?
When they filled the pen again – this was years later –
the train backed up, and an old woman
climbed on: she had waited all that time
to be rescued, or killed. She felt cheated,
for that strange diversion.
                    Where is she now?
Right here on this page, hiding in the ink you see.

WILLIAM STAFFORD

I AM A WRITER

I do not claim to be, I am a writer
as my passport insists
across decades, and still counting,
drawing humus from Year Twelve
when school bells added my name
to the throng gambolling along
with the Pied Piper of Hamelin
and, the Ancient Mariner
whose magic, and the bamboo flutes
of Martin Carter in Guyana jail,
took me by hand to know Ogun,
when Okigbo's road was famished.

I do not claim to be, I am a writer
as the crow flies, thrillingly sure
though the syllabus of errors
at the British High Commission
may set no column for my stripe
after mourned deaths of the mother
my waify poems at eighteen
elevate siblings at the WAEC
stocking ten-legged thesis
on muses who bring the unborn
to quaking life before stamps
hit the pad at the Passport Office.

I do not claim to be, I am a writer
whose trip under African skies
took Sun-dance to Sadler's Wells,
queen Elizabeth hall by the Thames,
and fleet street of glancing nods
with poesy of the body's rhythm
rounding the Cape of Good Hope
and toasting five hundred years
above visa-gripe and truth's fibre,
as art for life vouchsafes it,
setting navel closer to navel
to keep fellow-feeling in grace.

I do not claim to be, I am a writer
guerrilla-happy in unhappy times
pacing the common morality
of truth tougher than fear
and blood oaths segmenting worlds
and stalling the muse of spines
whose fist, raised in salute
to commonsense of hearts
to defeat spite and lucre
and the division of spoils
encumbering the earth with visas

I do not claim to be, I am a writer
beyond the prisonhouse of English

in which I wrest my djinns
I've crossed borders into Urdu,
and fished in the dialects of Rilke
world-round to tip my lagoon
in homage to Neruda's Spanish
I've returned gifts to Montale
wherever my English envy
denies a tongue its entry,
I'm happy, beyond mere fashion
for trips that visas can't deny

From *CANZONIERE*

1

O you who hear within these scattered verses
the sound of sighs with which I fed my heart
in my first errant youthful days when I
in part was not the man I am today;

for all the ways in which I weep and speak
between vain hopes, between vain suffering,
in anyone who knows love through its trials,
in them, may I find pity and forgiveness.

But now I see how I've become the talk
so long a time of people all around
(it often makes me feel so full of shame),

and from my vanities there comes shame's fruit,
and my repentance, and the clear awareness
that worldly joy is just a fleeting dream.

'TO WHOM SHALL I OFFER THIS BOOK?'

'To whom shall I offer this book, young and sprightly,
Neat, polished, wide-margined, and finished politely?
To you, my Cornelius, whose learning pedantic,
Has dared to set forth in three volumes gigantic
The history of ages – ye gods, what a labor! –
And still to enjoy the small wit of a neighbor.
A man who can be light and learned at once, sir,
By life's subtle logic is far from a dunce, sir.
So take my small book – if it meet with your favor,
The passing of years cannot dull its sweet savor.'

WHERE MY BOOKS GO

All the words that I gather
   And all the words that I write,
Must spread out their wings untiring,
   And never rest in their flight,
Till they come where your sad, sad heart is,
   And sing to you in the night,
Beyond where the waters are moving,
   Storm darkened or starry bright.

W. B. YEATS

THE AUTHOR TO HER BOOK

Thou ill-formed offspring of my feeble brain,
Who after birth didst by my side remain,
Till snatched from thence by friends less wise than
    true,
Who thee abroad exposed to public view,
Made thee in rags, halting to th' press to trudge,
Where errors were not lessened (all may judge).
At thy return my blushing was not small,
My rambling brat (in print) should mother call,
I cast thee by as one unfit for light,
Thy visage was so irksome in my sight;
Yet being mine own, at length affection would
Thy blemishes amend, if so I could.
I washed thy face, but more defects I saw,
And rubbing off a spot still made a flaw.
I stretched thy joints to make thee even feet,
Yet still thou run'st more hobbling than is meet;
In better dress to trim thee was my mind,
But nought save homespun cloth i' th' house I find.
In this array 'mongst vulgars may'st thou roam.
In critic's hands beware thou dost not come,
And take thy way where yet thou art not known;
If for thy father asked, say thou hadst none;
And for thy mother, she alas is poor,
Which caused her thus to send thee out of door.

EPIGRAMS I.3

So, they've summed you up, my little book.
You're now 'a milestone in ironic outlook.'
This the price of your publicity:
MARTIAL VIEWS LIFE VERY SAUCILY.
Whatever they say is a load of balls
Certain to send you to second-hand stalls,
Unaware, little book, of the comforts of home
Your 'low key wit' now belongs to Rome.
What today's 'an incandescent event'
Soon winds up 'a minor supplement.'
To set you off on the proper foot
Some shit's written 'Magic, a classic to boot.'

ODES III.30

EXEGI MONUMENTUM AERE PERENNIUS

This monument will outlast metal, and I made it
More durable than the king's seat, higher than
    pyramids.
Gnaw of the wind and rain? Impotent
The flow of years to break it, however many.
Bits of me, many bits, will dodge all funeral
Libitina/Persephone, and, after that,
Sprout new praise. As long as
Pontifex and the quiet girl pace the Capitol
I shall be spoken where the wild flood Aufidus
Lashes, and Daunus ruled the parched farmland:
Power from lowliness: 'First brought Aeolic song to
    Italian fashion' –
Wear pride, work's gain! O Muse Melpomene
By your will bind the laurel.
    My hair Delphic laurel.

      TRANSLATED BY EZRA POUND

SONNET XVIII

We are the sorry quills, bewildered, hurt,
The penknife and the little scissors too,
The petty instruments of sorrow who
Were used to write the words that you have heard.
Now we shall say what urged us to depart
From where we were and thus come here to you:
The hand that moved us spoke as if it knew
Of dreadful things appearing in the heart,
Which have undone him so he seems to be
Standing next door to death, a man who lives
With almost nothing left of him but sighs.
We pray you then, with all the strength we have:
Do not disdain to keep us till we see
At last some trace of pity in your eyes.

GUIDO CAVALCANTI   211
TRANSLATED BY ANTHONY MORTIMER

UNTITLED HAIKU

Today's moon;
will there be anyone
not taking up his pen?

UEJIMA ONITSURA
TRANSLATED BY R. H. BLYTH

AUTHORS

Over the meadows, and down the stream,
And through the garden-walks straying,
He plucks the flowers that fairest seem;
His throbbing heart brooks no delaying.
His maiden then comes – oh, what ecstasy!
Thy flowers thou giv'st for one glance of her eye!

The gard'ner next door o'er the hedge sees the youth:
'I'm not such a fool as that, in good truth;
My pleasure is ever to cherish each flower,
And see that no birds my fruit e'er devour.
But when 'tis ripe, your money, good neighbor!
'Twas not for nothing I took all this labor!'

And such, methinks, are the author-tribe.
The one his pleasures around him strews,
That his friends, the public, may reap, if they choose:
The other would fain make them all subscribe.

J. W. VON GOETHE   213
TRANSLATED BY EDGAR BOWRING

THE POET AND HIS SONGS

As the birds come in the Spring,
  We know not from where;
As the stars come at evening
  From depths of the air;

As the rain comes from the cloud,
  And the brook from the ground;
As suddenly, low or loud,
  Out of silence a sound;

As the grape comes to the vine,
  The fruit to the tree;
As the wind comes to the pine,
  And the tide to the sea;

As come the white sails of ships
  O'er the ocean's verge;
As comes the smile to the lips,
  The foam to the surge;

So come to the Poet his songs,
  All hitherward blown
From the misty realm, that belongs
  To the vast Unknown.

His, and not his, are the lays
   He sings; and their fame
Is his, and not his; and the praise
   And the pride of a name.

For voices pursue him by day,
   And haunt him by night,
And he listens, and needs must obey,
   When the Angel says: 'Write!'

'THE VERY FIRST TIME'

The very first time I sat down and put
a writing tablet on my lap, my own
Lykian Apollo said to me:
                                        'Make your sacrifice
as fat as you can, poet, but keep
your Muse on slender rations. And see that you go
where no hackneys plod: avoid the ruts
carved in the boulevard, even if it means
driving along a narrower path.'

MARGINALIA

BOOKWORMS: HOW TO KILL

There is a sort of busy worm
That will the fairest books deform,
  By gnawing holes throughout them;
Alike through ev'ry leaf they go,
Yet of its merits nought they know,
  Nor care they ought about them.

Their tasteless tooth will tear and taint
The poet, patriot, sage or saint,
  Nor sparing wit nor learning: –
Now if you'd know the reason why,
The best of reasons I'll supply –
  'Tis BREAD to the poor vermin.

Of pepper, snuff, or 'bacco-smoke,
And Russian-calf, they make a joke.
  Yet why should sons of Science
These puny, rankling reptiles dread –
'Tis but to let their books be read,
  And bid the worms defiance.

JOHN F. M. DOVASTON   219

THE BOOK-WORMS

[Burns wrote this reproof in a Shakspeare, which he found splendidly bound and gilt, but unread and worm-eaten, in a noble person's library.]

Through and through the inspir'd leaves,
    Ye maggots, make your windings;
But oh! respect his lordship's taste,
    And spare his golden bindings.

PAGE-EATER

Page-eater thou, the Muses' bitterest foe,
Hidden destroyer, feeding constantly
On stolen wisdom, why, black worm, lurk low
In holy works, emblem of jealousy?
Far from the Muses fly! And do not show
The envious tip of thy sharp probe to me –

[to which the following is the obvious reply:]

Quoth the bookworm 'I don't care a bit
If the writer has wisdom or wit.
   A volume must be
   Pretty tough to bore me
As completely as I can bore it.'

From *AURORA LEIGH*
(Book V)

[Aurora Leigh considers how she is to finance her trip to
Italy.]

I fear that I must sell this residue
Of my father's books, although the Elzevirs
Have fly-leaves overwritten by his hand
In faded notes as thick and fine and brown
As cobwebs on a tawny monument
Of the old Greeks – *conferenda haec cum his –*
Corruptè citat – lege potiùs,
And so on, in the scholar's regal way
Of giving judgment on the parts of speech,
As if he sat on all twelve thrones up-piled,
Arraigning Israel. Ay, but books and notes
Must go together. And this Proclus too,
In these dear quaint contracted Grecian types,
Fantastically crumpled like his thoughts
Which would not seem too plain; you go round twice
For one step forward, then you take it back
Because you're somewhat giddy; there's the rule
For Proclus. Ah, I stained this middle leaf
With pressing in't my Florence iris-bell,
Long stalk and all: my father chided me
For that stain of blue blood – I recollect

The peevish turn his voice took – 'Silly girls,
Who plant their flowers in our philosophy
To make it fine, and only spoil the book!
No more of it, Aurora.' 'Yes – no more!
Ah, blame of love, that's sweeter than all praise
Of those who love not! 'tis so lost to me,
I cannot, in such beggared life, afford
To lose my Proclus – not for Florence even.

BOOKMARKS

A bookmark for an album such as this,
Should be a ribbon with a cross-stitched phrase,
Pressed neatly into Milton's hymns of praise,
Yet here is none, but in this book of his,
That crossed the prairies with him long ago,
I find pale blades of buffalo grass to tell
Sweet pages where he could love Philomel,
And Phyllida and Cynthia and Chloe.
Here is a wedding song, stained by a leaf
Of mountain aspen, plucked when June was ripe;
If he marked other verse, I find no more,
But on one page, attuned to death and grief,
Are ashes from the embers of his pipe,
That must have spilled and did not reach the floor.

TO MY BOOKE-SELLER

Thou, that mak'st gaine thy end, and wisely well,
   Call'st a booke good, or bad, as it doth sell,
Use mine so, too: I give thee leave. But crave
   For the lucks sake, it thus much favour have,
To lye upon thy stall, till it be sought;
   Not offer'd, as it made sute to be bought;
Nor have my title-leafe on posts, or walls,
   Or in cleft-sticks, advanced to make calls
For termers, or some clarke-like serving-man,
   Who scarce can spell th'hard names: whose
       knight lesse can.
If, without these vile arts, it will not sell,
   Send it to *Bucklers-bury*, there 'twill, well.

THE SCENT OF OLD BOOKS

Strangely light
strangely sweet
strangely familiar
    and yet unknown
your fragrant memories
fill my heart
like the pleasant scent of
    old books.

TARANNUM RIYAZ
    TRANSLATED BY JAIPAL NANGIA

TO HIS BOOKE

Make haste away, and let one be
A friendly Patron unto thee:
Lest rapt from hence, I see thee lye
Torn for the use of Pasterie:
Or see thy injur'd Leaves serve well,
To make loose Gownes for Mackarell:
Or see the Grocers in a trice,
Make hoods of thee to serve out Spice.

BOOKS UP ON BOOKS

Color in Black, color in white
And also in different colors
Colors were brushed in minds
Respectively be hard

Printed embossed letters
In books of epigraphy
Color in black
On Space of white
Told that is black

Black white and colors
Books up on books
Being closed nearby
Dialogues having intercourse
Get soaked colors of minds
Smudged

Scabrous words
Boorish colors
In a content of
In a book
Wearing a strange cover

Not get closed
And be separated
Having filed up afar
At the library of old

On a table
Books up on books
Turn pages
Marking and conflicting
And also comparing

An empty paper
A pen
A hand with five fingers
An artist

'YOU'VE BOUGHT BOOKS'

You've bought books and filled shelves, O Lover of
    the Muses.
Does that mean you're a scholar now?
If you buy string instruments, plectrum and lyre
    today:
Do you think that by tomorrow the realm of music
    will be yours?

DECIMUS AUSONIUS
    TRANSLATED BY ALBERTO MANGRUEL

THE BIBLIOMANIAC'S PRAYER

Keep me, I pray, in wisdom's way
   That I may truths eternal seek;
I need protecting care to-day, –
   My purse is light, my flesh is weak.
So banish from my erring heart
   All baleful appetites and hints
Of Satan's fascinating art,
   Of first editions, and of prints.
Direct me in some godly walk
   Which leads away from bookish strife,
That I with pious deed and talk
   May extra-illustrate my life.

But if, O Lord, it pleaseth Thee
   To keep me in temptation's way,
I humbly ask that I may be
   Most notably beset to-day;
Let my temptation be a book,
   Which I shall purchase, hold, and keep,
Whereon when other men shall look,
   They 'll wail to know I got it cheap.
Oh, let it such a volume be
   As in rare copperplates abounds,
Large paper, clean, and fair to see,
   Uncut, unique, unknown to Lowndes.

EUGENE FIELD

BALLADE OF THE BOOK-MAN'S PARADISE

There *is* a Heaven, or here, or there, –
A Heaven there is, for me and you,
Where bargains meet for purses spare,
Like ours, are not so far and few.
Thuanus' bees go humming through
The learned groves, 'neath rainless skies,
O'er volumes old and volumes new,
Within that Book-man's Paradise!

There treasures bound for Longepierre
Keep brilliant their morocco blue,
There Hookes' *Amanda* is not rare,
Nor early tracts upon Peru!
Racine is common as Rotrou,
No Shakespeare Quarto search defies,
And Caxtons grow as blossoms grew,
Within that Book-man's Paradise!

There's Eve, – not our first mother fair, –
But Clovis Eve, a binder true;
Thither does Bauzonnet repair,
Derome, Le Gascon, Padeloup!
But never come the cropping crew
That dock a volume's honest size,

Nor they that 'letter' backs askew,
Within that Book-man's Paradise!

Friend, do not Heber and De Thou,
And Scott, and Southey, kind and wise,
La chasse au bouquin still pursue
Within that Book-man's Paradise?

ANDREW LANG   233

'I DON'T LIKE BOOKS'

I don't like books
as much
as Mallarmé seems
to have liked them
I'm not a book
and when people say
I really like your books
I wish I could say
like the poet Cesariny
listen
what I'd really like
is for you to like me
books aren't made
of flesh and blood
and when I feel
like crying
it doesn't help
to open a book
I need a hug
but thank God
the world isn't a book
and chance doesn't exist
still and all I really like
books
and believe in the Resurrection

of books
and believe that in Heaven
there are libraries
and reading and writing

ADÍLIA LOPES
TRANSLATED BY RICHARD ZENITH

SO MANY BOOKS
From *Fuente Ovejuna*

BARRILDO

So many books are published these days that every
Village square is full of self-proclaimed professors.

LEONELO

Yes, but has printing expanded or shrunk the sea
Of human knowledge? You know, I think the latter.
Ideas were once condensed in handy summaries
Today so much hot air is published, people get lost.
Try to keep abreast of everything that's printed
You get brain ache from information overload.
Only fools would deny that amongst all the dross,
Printing has made known the work of some great
    minds,
Preserved their thoughts against the ravages of
    time,
Spread their benevolent influence round the world:
But some poor souls, whose work was thought
    important
Have had their reputations destroyed by
    publication:
And some dishonest hacks have borrowed the name
Of our best playwright to get their work into print:
Whilst a few malicious souls have deliberately

Written rubbish and sent it out into the world
In the name of an enemy they seek to destroy!
Printing is not only a force for good, my friend.

LOPE DE VEGA 237
TRANSLATED BY LAURENCE BOSWELL

ECCLESIASTES 12:11–12

The sayings of the wise are like goads, and like nails firmly fixed are the collected sayings that are given by one shepherd.

Of anything beyond these, my child, beware. Of making many books there is no end, and much study is a weariness of the flesh.

A STUDY OF READING HABITS

When getting my nose in a book
Cured most things short of school,
It was worth ruining my eyes
To know I could still keep cool,
And deal out the old right hook
To dirty dogs twice my size.

Later, with inch-thick specs,
Evil was just my lark:
Me and my cloak and fangs
Had ripping times in the dark.
The women I clubbed with sex!
I broke them up like meringues.

Don't read much now: the dude
Who lets the girl down before
The hero arrives, the chap
Who's yellow and keeps the store,
Seem far too familiar. Get stewed:
Books are a load of crap.

RETHINKING BOOKS AND READING

BOOKSHOP STOPPING
After Philip Larkin's 'Church Going'

Once I'm convinced it's open, I go in,
No telling, after all, when one will close.
Attentive to the owner at her desk,
I smile and nod and shuffle by, not knowing,
As she completes our welcoming burlesque,
If she nods back in greeting or repose.

The mind blanks at this lair, where like a sty
From the last century, the vast, worm-eaten,
Usual used brigades of shabby *Babbitts*
And battered *Chatterleys* sprawl, bumped and beaten.
Man hands on mystery to man, that's why
This room's a study of dead reading habits.

Old fools with fragile jackets, broken spines,
A few, no doubt, unhinged, climb up the walls.
Intrigued, though, by some well-worn pickup lines –
A browser in a web till evening falls –
I read, enraptured, near a narrow aisle
And build my own small, reverential pile.

I page through to the only end of pages,
Then say 'The End' much louder than I'd meant.
Books are a load of scrap, I know, on shelves,

Best stay away and not have books ourselves.
No *screens* bear use by hands from other ages
To hint we'll go, as prior owners went.

When libraries and bookshops disappear,
And scanners hold our poetry and prose,
A large cool Apple store is planted here,
And volumes aren't part of the equation,
Will someone, stopping in, acquire, unplanned,
An early e-book version of *Persuasion?*

Will books live on as little household gods
When they have yellowed into mounds of silt?
Who knows? Not me. The best that I can muster
On everybody's future hopes and odds,
As I slink out with bags of books and guilt,
Is that, at least, we've all outlived Blockbuster.

DECEMBER'S DOOR
in memoriam Philip Larkin

I kept a church leaf, wishing it were blossom.
   Hull's undressed roadside sycamores
Waded through brittle drifts from Cottingham
   To Newland Park, the still striders.
That leaf still marks my place, but it was worn
   Before I put it there; now dust
Dirties the page, and sinews, strong as thorn,
   Impress the paper's softer crust,
Fragments hanging from them, leaves of a leaf
   Preserved into a second autumn.
Afterwards' keepsake, its botanic grief
   Crumbles in death's *ad infinitum.*

A rudimentary, unclouded sky:
   That day in Hull, your funeral,
I watched rubescent figments vitrify
   On library windows, unreal
Emblems of warehoused English literature
   On the Fifth Floor, and saw again –
When I was in my twenties, I worked there –
   Hull's hazily Utopian green
Purpled and pinkened in a luminous
   Record of seasons. Long straight roads

Reached out across nocturnal Holderness,
    The sea and the visitless woods.

A leaf-marked book aches on my windowsill.
    Straw gold and central green were there
A year ago, but book-locked winterkill
    Disfigured them in printed air.
In a closed shadow, opened now, a door
    Into December's estuary
Beneath a wigged moon, it honeys the floor
    To starry oak, reflected Tay.
Geese draw their audible, Siberian bow
    Over the moon and Buddon Ness,
And now I can't repay the debt I owe,
    A withered leaf, a dry distress.

Sorrow's vernacular, its minimum,
    A leaf brought in on someone's shoe
Gatecrashed the church in muffled Cottingham,
    Being's late gift, its secret value
A matter of downtrodden poetry,
    Diminutive, and brought to this
By luck of lyric and an unknown tree.
    A passer-by was bound to notice
Crisp leaves at work when everyone had gone,
    Some fricative on paving-stones
As others flecked a winter-wrinkled lawn,
    Remote, unswept oblivions.

THE AFTERLIFE OF LIBRARIES

When the shelves are dismantled, the visitations
       begin,
brief ghostly apparitions of recycled volumes
in a remote corner of the upper stacks

where the Qs were, crowded but less
visited than some of the more welcoming books,
the ones down in the Ps unburdened by a tumult

of formulas, the deltas and thetas
that are just Greek to students who spend
more time daydreaming than doing labs.

There, above the reinforced concrete floor
that supported the old weight of knowledge,
in the red glow of the Exit signs, the lost

empirical tomes assert their quantum prerogative
to flicker back into existence for a picosecond
and to shed their complex words into the mute air

riddled with signals, the layered protocols running
on staggered frequencies and bearing the disembodied
syllables that could be the soul of thought.

Unexplained interferences start to interrupt
the dependable performance of mobile devices,
a perfect storm of untethered content appearing

in fragments on bright sharp touch screens
where people see their faces reflected as background
to whatever they read. A woman looking at
        weather.com

has several sentences on Analysis of Variance
inserted at the bottom of her display, just above
the navigation icons. A guy using his golf GPS app

gets equations defining the photoelectric effect
overlaid on a contour map of the seventh green.
A kid playing Pokemon online is puzzled

by the description of glutamine synthesis
scrawled across the gym floor. It happens at random,
this networked dispersion of facts and discourse

into the cellular ether where people graze
bits of information they need for a minute
without realizing the matrix of mind and culture

has been un-housed and rendered formless, and flows
now through buildings, over mountains and rivers
without destination, without an endpoint

in the binding physical artifact that is its past perfect
home. But information wants to be more than free.
It wants to matter and last, to counter entropy

with the order of classified things, as if blooming
out of the multi-verse there could in fact be pure
        forms,
ideal manifestations of all the ways we know

revealed in what we held as books but what are
        instead
in this altered place shadow beings from a gone world,
a world where fingers made a tacit pact with signs

pressed into paper: that we can embrace thought
and witness its slow accretion, that we can take
pleasure or solace in the long corridors full

of others' words that enlighten and humble us.
        Suddenly
it seems there's a corrective impulse in the curled up
dimensions at the Planck distance, the hidden-then-
        revealed

bridges across unmeasured magnitudes
of space and time: hints that the old collections persist
somewhere and foam up into being again here,

breaking through the welter of digital distractions,
giving hope to those who remember the weight of
      pages
and the contract with the future of a few strong words

emblazoned on all the various and durable spines.

THE BOOK BURNINGS

When the regime ordered that books with harmful
    knowledge
Should be publicly burnt, and all around
Oxen were forced to drag cartloads of books
To the pyre, one banished poet
One of the best, discovered, studying the list of the
    burnt
To his horror, that his books
Had been forgotten. He hurried to his desk
On wings of rage and wrote a letter to the powers
    that be.
Burn me! he wrote, his pen flying, burn me!
Don't do this to me! Don't pass me over! Have I not
    always told
The truth in my books? And now
I am treated by you as a liar!
                     I order you:
Burn me!

BERTOLT BRECHT   251
TRANSLATED BY TOM KUHN

THE FUTURE OF BOOKS

Or this: some sci-fi aeon where a drill
draws out a deep core sample,
a candy stick of sands and clays,
each civilization, the gist of all its stories,
packed into a slab of sediment.
Our slice has its own distinctive shade and scent
– paper-musk, the dark behind bookshelves –
but it so mystifies our future selves
they fry it like black pudding, a salt and bitter
jus of atlas, sonnet, gossip, scripture.
Text is long gone, adrift in virtual vaults
with mislaid passcodes. Think of bottles
on a cyber-tide, never breaking shore,
bearing love letters for strangers.

THE LIBRARIES DIDN'T BURN

despite books kindled in electronic flames.

The locket of bookish love
still opens and shuts.

But its words have migrated
to a luminous elsewhere.

Neither completely oral nor written —
a somewhere in between.

Then will oak, willow,
birch, and olive poets return
to their digital tribes —

trees wander back to the forest?

INDEX OF AUTHORS

258

ACKNOWLEDGMENTS

Thanks are due to the following copyright holders for permission to reprint:

JULIA ALVAREZ: 'Waiting for My Father to Pick Me Up at the Library' from *The Woman I Kept to Myself*. Reprinted with the permission of Susan Bergholz Agency. YURI ANDRUKHOVYCH: 'Library' (tr. Virlana Tkacz and Wanda Phipps) from *A Hundred Years of Youth: A Bilingual Anthology of 20th Century Ukrainian* Poetry, ed. Olha Luchuk and Michael M. Naydan (Litopys, Lviv, 2000). Reprinted with permission of the poet. MAYA ANGELOU: 'I Love the Look of Words' by Maya Angelou, copyright © 1993 by Maya Angelou; from *Souls Look Back in Wonder* by Tom Feelings. Used by permission of Dial Books for Young Readers, an imprint of Penguin Young Readers Group, a division of Penguin Random House LLC. All rights reserved. W. H. AUDEN: 'Montaigne' copyright 1945 by W. H. Auden. Copyright © renewed 1973 by The Estate of W. H. Auden; from *Collected Poems* by W. H. Auden, edited by Edward Mendelson. Used by permission of Random House, an imprint and division of Penguin Random House LLC. All rights reserved. Curtis Brown US. DECIMUS AUSONIUS: 'You've bought books' translated by Alberto Manguel, from *History of Reading*, HarperCollins, 1996. HILAIRE BELLOC: 'On His Books' from *The Augustan Books of Modern Poetry: Hilaire Belloc*. Peters, Fraser & Dunlop. GIOVANNI BOCCACCIO: 'Boccaccio Sends Petrarch a Copy of Dante' translated by David Thompson. Reprinted with the kind permission of Alan F. Nagel. Copyright © 1971 by David Thompson. JORGE LUIS BORGES: 'On Acquiring an Encyclopedia', translated by Alan S. Trueblood from *Selected Poems* (bilingual edition), ed. Alexander Coleman, Penguin, 1999. BERTOLT BRECHT: 'The Book Burnings' (tr. Tom Kuhn) from *The Collected Poems of Bertolt Brecht*, translated by David Constantine and Tom Kuhn. Liveright Publishing Corporation, 2018. JOSEPH BRODSKY: from 'Elegy for John Donne'. Joseph Brodsky Memorial Society. FREDERICK BUECHNER: 'The Mystery of Words' from *A*

267

the Governing Empires (Shearsman, 2010). Reprinted with permission from Shearsman Books. LAURIE L. PATTON: 'On Learning a Sacred Language in Childhood', first printed in a slightly different form in Laurie L. Patton, *Fire's Goal: Poems from a Hindu Year*, White Clouds Press, 2003. PETRARCH: poem 1 of the *Canzoniere*, from *Petrarch: The Canzoniere, or, Rerum vulgarium fragmenta*, translated into Verse with Notes and a Commentary by Mark Musa, Indiana University Press, 1996. EZRA POUND: 'Cantico del Sole' by Ezra Pound, from *Personae*, copyright © 1926 by Ezra Pound. Reprinted by permission of New Directions Publishing Corp. Published by Faber & Faber Ltd. Reprinted with permission. LYNN POWELL: 'Sword Drill' originally published in *Old and New Testaments* by Lynn Powell © 1995 by the Board of Regents of the University of Wisconsin System. Reprinted by permission of the University of Wisconsin Press. All rights reserved. MEL PRYOR: 'In a Secondhand Bookshop'. Reprinted with permission from the poet. TESSA RANSFORD: Excerpt from 'In Praise of Libraries' from *When It Works It Feels Like Play*, Ramsay Press, Edinburgh, 1998. Reprinted with permission from the Estate of Tessa Ransford. ALBERTO RÍOS: 'Don't Go into the Library'. Copyright © by Alberto Ríos. Reprinted with permission of the poet. TARANNUM RIYAZ: 'The Scent of Old Books' translated by Jaipal Nangia from *Indian Literature* (Vol. XL VII No. 3). Sahitya Akademi, 2003. MICHAEL SYMMONS ROBERTS: 'The Future of Books' from *Mancunia*, reprinted with permission from United Agents. Jonathan Cape. JUAN MANUEL ROCA: 'The Library of the Blind', translated by Raúl Jaime Gaviria, from *Luna de Ciegos* (University of Antioquia, 1991). FLAVIO SANTI: 'Dear Mary' translated by Gabriele Poole. Copyright © 2004 by Flavio Santi. Reprinted with the permission of the poet. Translation copyright © 2004 by Gabriele Poole. Reprinted with permission from Gabriel Poole. SIEGFRIED SASSOON: 'To an Eighteenth Century Poet'. Published by Faber & Faber Ltd. Copyright Siegfried Sasson. Reprinted by kind permission of the Estate of George Sassoon. GJERTRUD SCHNACKENBERG: 'Supernatural Love' from *Supernatural Love: Poems 1976–1992*, Farrar, Straus & Giroux,

271

272